Getting Real

The smarter, faster, easier way to build a successful web application

First edition
ISBN 978-0-578-01281-0

Contents

Feature Selection

Process

The Organization

Staffing

Interface Design

Code

Words

Pricing and Signup

Promotion

Introduction

What is Getting Real?

Want to build a successful web app? Then it's time to Get Real. Getting Real is a smaller, faster, better way to build software.

Getting Real is about skipping all the stuff that *represents* real (charts, graphs, boxes, arrows, schematics, wireframes, etc.) and *actually building the real thing*.

Getting real is less. Less mass, less software, less features, less paperwork, less of everything that's not essential (and most of what you think is essential actually isn't).

Getting Real is staying small and being agile.

Getting Real starts with the interface, the real screens that people are going to use. It begins with what the customer actually experiences and builds backwards from there. This lets you get the interface right before you get the software wrong.

Getting Real is about iterations and lowering the cost of change. Getting Real is all about launching, tweaking, and constantly improving which makes it a perfect approach for web-based software.

Getting Real delivers just what customers need and eliminates anything they don't.

The benefits of Getting Real

Getting Real delivers better results because it forces you to deal with the actual problems you're trying to solve instead of your ideas about those problems. It forces you to deal with reality.

Getting Real foregoes functional specs and other transitory documentation in favor of building real screens. A functional spec is make-believe, an illusion of agreement, while an actual web page is reality. That's what your customers are going to see and use. That's what matters. Getting Real gets you there faster. And that means you're making software decisions based on the real thing instead of abstract notions.

Finally, Getting Real is an approach ideally suited to web-based software. The old school model of shipping software in a box and then waiting a year or two to deliver an update is fading away. Unlike installed software, web apps can constantly evolve on a day-to-day basis. Getting Real leverages this advantage for all its worth.

How To Write Vigorous Software

Vigorous writing is concise. A sentence should contain no unnecessary words, a paragraph no unnecessary sentences, for the same reason that a drawing should have no unnecessary lines and a machine no unnecessary parts. This requires not that the writer make all sentences short or avoid all detail and treat subjects only in outline, but that every word tell.

From "The Elements of Style" by William Strunk Jr.

No more bloat

The old way: a lengthy, bureaucratic, we're-doing-this-to-cover-our-asses process. The typical result: bloated, forgettable software dripping with mediocrity. Blech.

Getting Real gets rid of...

Timelines that take months or even years

Pie-in-the-sky functional specs

Scalability debates

Interminable staff meetings

The "need" to hire dozens of employees

Meaningless version numbers

Pristine roadmaps that predict the perfect future

Endless preference options

Outsourced support

Unrealistic user testing

Useless paperwork

Top-down hierarchy

You don't need tons of money or a huge team or a lengthy development cycle to build great software. Those things are the ingredients for slow, murky, changeless applications. Getting real takes the opposite approach.

In this book we'll show you...

The importance of having a philosophy

Why staying small is a good thing

How to build less

How to get from idea to reality quickly

How to staff your team

Why you should design from the inside out

Why writing is so crucial

Why you should underdo your competition

How to promote your app and spread the word

Secrets to successful support

Tips on keeping momentum going after launch

...and lots more

The focus is on big-picture ideas. We won't bog you down with detailed code snippets or CSS tricks. We'll stick to the major ideas and philosophies that drive the Getting Real process.

Is this book for you?

You're an entrepreneur, designer, programmer, or marketer working on a big idea.

You realize the old rules don't apply anymore. Distribute your software on CD-ROMS every year? How 2002. Version numbers? Out the window. You need to build, launch, and tweak. Then rinse and repeat.

Or maybe you're not yet on board with agile development and business structures, but you're eager to learn more.

If this sounds like you, then this book is for you.

Note: While this book's emphasis is on building a web app, a lot of these ideas are applicable to non-software activities too. The suggestions about small teams, rapid prototyping, expecting iterations, and many others presented here can serve as a guide whether you're starting a business, writing a book, designing a web site, recording an album, or doing a variety of other endeavors. Once you start Getting Real in one area of your life, you'll see how these concepts can apply to a wide range of activities.

About 37signals

What we do

37signals is a small team that creates simple, focused software. Our products help you collaborate and get organized. More than 500,000 people and small businesses use our web-apps to get things done. Jeremy Wagstaff, of the Wall Street Journal, wrote, "37signals products are beautifully simple, elegant and intuitive tools that make an Outlook screen look like the software equivalent of a torture chamber." Our apps never put you on the rack.

Our modus operandi

We believe software is too complex. Too many features, too many buttons, too much to learn. Our products do less than the competition – intentionally. We build products that work smarter, feel better, allow you to do things your way, and are easier to use.

Our products

As of the publishing date of this book, we have five commercial products and one open source web application framework.

Basecamp turns project management on its head. Instead of Gantt charts, fancy graphs, and stats-heavy spreadsheets, Basecamp offers message boards, to-do lists, simple scheduling, collaborative writing, and file sharing. So far, hundreds of thousands agree it's a better way. Farhad Manjoo of Salon.com said "Basecamp represents the future of software on the Web."

Campfire brings simple group chat to the business setting. Businesses in the know understand how valuable real-time persistent group chat can be. Conventional instant messaging is great for quick 1-on-1 chats, but it's miserable for 3 or more people at once. Campfire solves that problem and plenty more.

Backpack is the alternative to those confusing, complex, "organize your life in 25 simple steps" personal information managers. Backpack's simple take on pages, notes, to-dos, and cellphone/email-based reminders is a novel idea in a product category that suffers from status-quo-itis. Thomas Weber of the Wall Street Journal said it's the best product in its class and David Pogue of the New York Times called it a "very cool" organization tool.

Writeboard lets you write, share, revise, and compare text solo or with others. It's the refreshing alternative to bloated word processors that are overkill for 95% of what you write. John Gruber of Daring Fireball said, "Writeboard might be the clearest, simplest web application I've ever seen." Web-guru Jeffrey Zeldman said, "The brilliant minds at 37signals have done it again."

Ta-da List keeps all your to-do lists together and organized online. Keep the lists to yourself or share them with others for easy collaboration. There's no easier way to get things done. Over 200,000 lists with over 2,000,000 items have been created so far.

Ruby on Rails, for developers, is a full-stack, open-source web framework in Ruby for writing real-world applications quickly and easily. Rails takes care of the busy work so you can focus on your idea. Nathan Torkington of the O'Reilly publishing empire said "Ruby on Rails is astounding. Using it is like watching a kung-fu movie, where a dozen bad-ass frameworks prepare to beat up the little newcomer only to be handed their asses in a variety of imaginative ways." Gotta love that quote.

You can find our more about our products and our company on our web site at: http://www.37signals.com.

Caveats, disclaimers, and other preemptive strikes

Just to get it out of the way, here are our responses to some complaints we hear every now and again:

"These techniques won't work for me."

Getting real is a system that's worked terrifically for us. That said, the ideas in this book won't apply to every project under the sun. If you are building a weapons system, a nuclear control plant, a banking system for millions of customers, or some other life/finance-critical system, you're going to balk at some of our laissez-faire attitude. Go ahead and take additional precautions.

And it doesn't have to be an all or nothing proposition. Even if you can't embrace Getting Real fully, there are bound to be at least a few ideas in here you can sneak past the powers that be.

"You didn't invent that idea."

We're not claiming to have invented these techniques. Many of these concepts have been around in one form or another for a long time. Don't get huffy if you read some of our advice and it reminds you of something you read about already on so and so's weblog or in some book published 20 years ago. It's definitely possible. These techniques are not at all exclusive to 37signals. We're just telling you how we work and what's been successful for us.

"You take too much of a black and white view."

If our tone seems too know-it-allish, bear with us. We think it's better to present ideas in bold strokes than to be wishy-washy about it. If that comes off as cocky or arrogant, so be it. We'd rather be provocative than water everything down with "it depends..." Of course there will be times when these rules need to be stretched or broken. And some of these tactics may not apply to your situation. Use your judgement and imagination.

"This won't work inside my company."

Think you're too big to Get Real? Even Microsoft is Getting Real (and we doubt you're bigger than them). Google follows many of these principles as well.

Even if your company typically runs on long-term schedules with big teams, there are still ways to get real. The first step is to break up into smaller units. When there's too many people involved, nothing gets done. The leaner you are, the faster – and better – things get done.

Granted, it may take some salesmanship. Pitch your company on the Getting Real process. Show them this book. Show them the real results you can achieve in less time and with a smaller team.

Explain that Getting Real is a low-risk, low-investment way to test new concepts. See if you can split off from the mothership on a smaller project as a proof of concept. Demonstrate results.

Or, if you really want to be ballsy, go stealth. Fly under the radar and demonstrate real results. That's the approach the Start.com team has used while Getting Real at Microsoft. "I've watched the Start.com team work. They don't ask permission," says Robert Scoble, Technical Evangelist at Microsoft. "They have a boss that provides air cover. And they bite off a little bit at a time and do that and respond to feedback."

Shipping Microsoft's Start.com

In big companies, processes and meetings are the norm.
Many months are spent on planning features and arguing
details with the goal of everyone reaching an agreement
on what is the "right" thing for the customer.

That may be the right approach for shrink-wrapped software, but
with the web we have an incredible advantage. Just ship it! Let the
user tell you if it's the right thing and if it's not, hey you can fix it
and ship it to the web the same day if you want! There is no word
stronger than the customer's – resist the urge to engage in long-
winded meetings and arguments. Just ship it and prove a point.

Much easier said than done – this implies:

Months of planning are not necessary.
Months of writing specs are not necessary – specs should have
the foundations nailed and details figured out and refined
during the development phase. Don't try to close all open issues
and nail every single detail before development starts.

Ship less features, but quality features.
You don't need a big bang approach with a whole new release and
bunch of features. Give the users byte-size pieces that they can digest.

If there are minor bugs, ship it as soon you have the core scenarios
nailed and ship the bug fixes to web gradually after that. The faster
you get the user feedback the better. Ideas can sound great on paper
but in practice turn out to be suboptimal. The sooner you find out
about fundamental issues that are wrong with an idea, the better.

Once you iterate quickly and react on customer feedback, you
will establish a customer connection. Remember the goal
is to win the customer by building what they want.

-Sanaz Ahari, Program Manager of Start.com, Microsoft

The Starting Line

Build Less

Underdo your competition

Conventional wisdom says that to beat your competitors you need to one-up them. If they have four features, you need five (or 15, or 25). If they're spending x, you need to spend xx. If they have 20, you need 30.

This sort of one-upping Cold War mentality is a dead-end. It's an expensive, defensive, and paranoid way of building products. Defensive, paranoid companies can't think ahead, they can only think behind. They don't lead, they follow.

If you want to build a company that follows, you might as well put down this book now.

So what to do then? The answer is less. Do less than your competitors to beat them. Solve the simple problems and leave the hairy, difficult, nasty problems to everyone else. Instead of one-upping, try one-downing. Instead of outdoing, try underdoing.

We'll cover the concept of less throughout this book, but for starters, less means:

Less features
Less options/preferences
Less people and corporate structure
Less meetings and abstractions
Less promises

What's Your Problem?

Build software for yourself

A great way to build software is to start out by solving your own problems. You'll be the target audience and you'll know what's important and what's not. That gives you a great head start on delivering a breakout product.

The key here is understanding that you're not alone. If you're having this problem, it's likely hundreds of thousands of others are in the same boat. There's your market. Wasn't that easy?

Basecamp originated in a problem: As a design firm we needed a simple way to communicate with our clients about projects. We started out doing this via client extranets which we would update manually. But changing the HTML by hand every time a project needed to be updated just wasn't working. These project sites always seemed to go stale and eventually were abandoned. It was frustrating because it left us disorganized and left clients in the dark.

So we started looking at other options. Yet every tool we found either 1) didn't do what we needed or 2) was bloated with features we didn't need – like billing, strict access controls, charts, graphs, etc. We knew there had to be a better way so we decided to build our own.

When you solve your own problem, you create a tool that you're passionate about. And passion is key. Passion means you'll truly use it and care about it. And that's the best way to get others to feel passionate about it too.

Scratching your own itch

The Open Source world embraced this mantra a long time ago – they call it "scratching your own itch." For the open source developers, it means they get the tools they want, delivered the way they want them. But the benefit goes much deeper.

As the designer or developer of a new application, you're faced with hundreds of micro-decisions each and every day: blue or green? One table or two? Static or dynamic? Abort or recover? How do we make these decisions? If it's something we recognize as being important, we might ask. The rest, we guess. And all that guessing builds up a kind of debt in our applications – an interconnected web of assumptions.

As a developer, I hate this. The knowledge of all these small-scale timebombs in the applications I write adds to my stress. Open Source developers, scratching their own itches, don't suffer this. Because they are their own users, they know the correct answers to 90% of the decisions they have to make. I think this is one of the reasons folks come home after a hard day of coding and then work on open source: It's relaxing.

–Dave Thomas, The Pragmatic Programmers

Born out of necessity

Campaign Monitor really was born out of necessity. For years we'd been frustrated by the quality of the email marketing options out there. One tool would do x and y but never z, the next had y and z nailed but just couldn't get x right. We couldn't win.

We decided to clear our schedule and have a go at building our dream email marketing tool. We consciously decided not to look at what everyone else was doing and instead build something that would make ours and our customer's lives a little easier.

As it turned out, we weren't the only ones who were unhappy with the options out there. We made a few modifications to the software so any design firm could use it and started spreading the word. In less than six months, thousands of designers were using Campaign Monitor to send email newsletters for themselves and their clients.

–David Greiner, founder, Campaign Monitor

You need to care about it

When you write a book, you need to have more than an interesting story. You need to have a desire to tell the story. You need to be personally invested in some way. If you're going to live with something for two years, three years, the rest of your life, you need to care about it.

–Malcolm Gladwell, author (from A Few Thin Slices of Malcolm Gladwell)

Fund Yourself

Outside money is plan B

The first priority of many startups is acquiring funding from investors. But remember, if you turn to outsiders for funding, you'll have to answer to them too. Expectations are raised. Investors want their money back – and quickly. The sad fact is cashing in often begins to trump building a quality product.

These days it doesn't take much to get rolling. Hardware is cheap and plenty of great infrastructure software is open source and free. And passion doesn't come with a price tag.

So do what you can with the cash on hand. Think hard and determine what's really essential and what you can do without. What can you do with three people instead of ten? What can you do with $20K instead of $100K? What can you do in three months instead of six? What can you do if you keep your day job and build your app on the side?

Constraints force creativity

Run on limited resources and you'll be forced to reckon with constraints earlier and more intensely. And that's a good thing. Constraints drive innovation.

Constraints also force you to get your idea out in the wild sooner rather than later – another good thing. A month or two out of the gates you should have a pretty good idea of whether you're onto something or not. If you are, you'll be self-sustainable shortly and won't need external cash. If your idea's a lemon, it's time to go back to the drawing board. At least you know now as opposed to months (or years) down the road. And at least you can back out easily. Exit plans get a lot trickier once investors are involved.

If you're creating software just to make a quick buck, it will show. Truth is a quick payout is pretty unlikely. So focus on building a quality tool that you and your customers can live with for a long time.

Two paths

[Jake Walker started one company with investor money (Disclive) and one without (The Show). Here he discusses the differences between the two paths.]

The root of all the problems wasn't raising money itself, but everything that came along with it. The expectations are simply higher. People start taking salary, and the motivation is to build it up and sell it, or find some other way for the initial investors to make their money back. In the case of the first company, we simply started acting much bigger than we were – out of necessity...

[With The Show] we realized that we could deliver a much better product with less costs, only with more time. And we gambled with a bit of our own money that people would be willing to wait for quality over speed. But the company has stayed (and will likely continue to be) a small operation. And ever since that first project, we've been fully self funded. With just a bit of creative terms from our vendors, we've never really need to put much of our own money into the operation at all. And the expectation isn't to grow and sell, but to grow for the sake of growth and to continue to benefit from it financially.

–A comment from Signal vs. Noise

Fix Time and Budget, Flex Scope

Launch on time and on budget

Here's an easy way to launch on time and on budget: keep them fixed. Never throw more time or money at a problem, just scale back the scope.

There's a myth that goes like this: we can launch on time, on budget, and on scope. It almost never happens and when it does quality often suffers.

If you can't fit everything in within the time and budget allotted then don't expand the time and budget. Instead, pull back the scope. There's always time to add stuff later – later is eternal, now is fleeting.

Launching something great that's a little smaller in scope than planned is better than launching something mediocre and full of holes because you had to hit some magical time, budget, and scope window. Leave the magic to Houdini. You've got a real business to run and a real product to deliver.

Here are the benefits of fixing time and budget, and keeping scope flexible:

Prioritization
You have to figure out what's really important. What's going to make it into this initial release? This forces a constraint on you which will push you to make tough decisions instead of hemming and hawing.

Reality

Setting expectations is key. If you try to fix time, budget, and scope, you won't be able to deliver at a high level of quality. Sure, you can probably deliver something, but is "something" what you really want to deliver?

Flexibility

The ability to change is key. Having everything fixed makes it tough to change. Injecting scope flexibility will introduce options based on your real experience building the product. Flexibility is your friend.

Our recommendation: Scope down. It's better to make half a product than a half-assed product (more on this later).

One, two, three...

How does a project get to be a year behind schedule? One day at a time.

-Fred Brooks, software engineer and computer scientist

Have an Enemy

Pick a fight

Sometimes the best way to know what your app should be is to know what it shouldn't be. Figure out your app's enemy and you'll shine a light on where you need to go.

When we decided to create project management software, we knew Microsoft Project was the gorilla in the room. Instead of fearing the gorilla, we used it as a motivator. We decided Basecamp would be something completely different, the anti-Project.

We realized project management isn't about charts, graphs, reports and statistics – it's about communication. It also isn't about a project manager sitting up high and broadcasting a project plan. It's about everyone taking responsibility together to make the project work.

Our enemy was the Project Management Dictators and the tools they used to crack the whip. We wanted to democratize project management – make it something everyone was a part of (including the client). Projects turn out better when everyone takes collective ownership of the process.

When it came to Writeboard, we knew there were competitors out there with lots of whizbang features. So we decided to emphasize a "no fuss" angle instead. We created an app that let people share and collaborate on ideas simply, without bogging them down with non-essential features. If it wasn't essential, we left it out. And in just three months after launch, over 100,000 Writeboards have been created.

When we started on Backpack our enemy was structure and rigid rules. People should be able to organize their information their own way – not based on a series of preformatted screens or a plethora of required form fields.

One bonus you get from having an enemy is a very clear marketing message. People are stoked by conflict. And they also understand a product by comparing it to others. With a chosen enemy, you're feeding people a story they want to hear. Not only will they understand your product better and faster, they'll take sides. And that's a sure-fire way to get attention and ignite passion.

Now with all that said, it's also important to not get too obsessed with the competition. Overanalyze other products and you'll start to limit the way you think. Take a look and then move on to your own vision and your own ideas.

Don't follow the leader

Marketers (and all human beings) are well trained to follow the leader. The natural instinct is to figure out what's working for the competition and then try to outdo it – to be cheaper than your competitor who competes on price, or faster than the competitor who competes on speed. The problem is that once a consumer has bought someone else's story and believes that lie, persuading the consumer to switch is the same as persuading him to admit he was wrong. And people hate admitting that they're wrong.

Instead, you must tell a different story and persuade listeners that your story is more important than the story they currently believe. If your competition is faster, you must be cheaper. If they sell the story of health, you must sell the story of convenience. Not just the positioning x/y axis sort of "We are cheaper" claim, but a real story that is completely different from the story that's already being told.

–Seth Godin, author/entrepreneur (from Be a Better Liar)

What's the key problem?

One of the quickest ways to get yourself into trouble is to look at what your competitors are doing. This has been especially true for us at BlinkList. Since we launched there have been about 10 other social bookmarking services that have been launched. Some people have even started to generate spreadsheets online with a detailed feature by feature comparison.

However, this can quickly lead one astray. Instead, we stay focused on the big picture and keep asking ourselves, what is the key problem we are trying to solve and how can we solve it.

–Michael Reining, co-founder, MindValley & Blinklist

It Shouldn't be a Chore

Your passion – or lack of – will shine through

The less your app is a chore to build, the better it will be. Keep it small and managable so you can actually enjoy the process.

If your app doesn't excite you, something's wrong. If you're only working on it in order to cash out, it will show. Likewise, if you feel passionately about your app, it will come through in the final product. People can read between the lines.

The presence of passion

In design, where meaning is often controversially subjective or painfully inscrutable, few things are more apparent and lucid than the presence of passion. This is true whether the design of a product delights you or leaves you cold; in either case it's difficult not to detect the emotional investment of the hands that built it.

Enthusiasm manifests itself readily of course, but indifference is equally indelible. If your commitment doesn't encompass a genuine passion for the work at hand, it becomes a void that is almost impossible to conceal, no matter how elaborately or attractively designed it is.

–Khoi Vinh, Subtraction.com and co-founder of Behavior LLC

The bakery

American business at this point is really about developing an idea, making it profitable, selling it while it's profitable and then getting out or diversifying. It's just about sucking everything up. My idea was: Enjoy baking, sell your bread, people like it, sell more. Keep the bakery going because you're making good food and people are happy.

–Ian MacKaye, member of Fugazi and co-owner of Dischord Records
(from Salon.com People | Ian MacKaye)

Stay Lean

Less Mass

The leaner you are, the easier it is to change

The more massive an object, the more energy is required to change its direction. It's as true in the business world as it is in the physical world.

When it comes to web technology, change must be easy and cheap. If you can't change on the fly, you'll lose ground to someone who can. That's why you need to shoot for less mass.

Mass is increased by...

Long term contracts

Excess staff

Permanent decisions

Meetings about other meetings

Thick process

Inventory (physical or mental)

Hardware, software, technology lock-ins

Proprietary data formats

The past ruling the future

Long-term roadmaps

Office politics

Mass is reduced by...

Just-in-time thinking

Multi-tasking team members

Embracing constraints, not trying to lift them

Less software, less code

Less features

Small team size

Simplicity

Pared-down interfaces

Open-source products

Open data formats

An open culture that makes it easy to admit mistakes

Less mass lets you change direction quickly. You can react and evolve. You can focus on the good ideas and drop the bad ones. You can listen and respond to your customers. You can integrate new technologies now instead of later. Instead of an aircraft carrier, you steer a cigarette boat. Revel in that fact.

For example, let's imagine a lean, less mass company that has built a product with less software and less features. On the other side is a more mass company that's got a product with significantly more software and more features. Then let's say a new technology like Ajax or a new concept like tagging comes around. Who is going to be able to adapt their product quicker? The team with more software and more features and a 12-month roadmap or the team with less software and less features and a more organic "let's focus on what we need to focus on right now" process?

Obviously the less-mass company is in a better position to adjust to the real demands of the marketplace. The more-mass company will likely still be discussing changes or pushing them through its bureaucratic process long after the less-mass company has made the switch. The less mass company will be two steps ahead while the more mass company is still figuring out how to walk.

Nimble, agile, less-mass businesses can quickly change their entire business model, product, feature set, and marketing message. They can make mistakes and fix them quickly. They can change their priorities, product mix, and focus. And, most importantly, **they can change their minds**.

Lower Your Cost of Change

Stay flexible by reducing obstacles to change

Change is your best friend. The more expensive it is to make a change, the less likely you'll make it. And if your competitors can change faster than you, you're at a huge disadvantage. If change gets too expensive, you're dead.

Here's where staying lean really helps you out. The ability to change on a dime is one thing small teams have by default that big teams can never have. This is where the big guys envy the little guys. What might take a big team in a huge organization weeks to change may only take a day in a small, lean organization. That advantage is price-less. Cheap and fast changes are small's secret weapon.

And remember: All the cash, all the marketing, all the people in the world can't buy the agility you get from being small.

Emergence

Emergence is one of the founding principles of agility, and is the closest one to pure magic. Emergent properties aren't designed or built in, they simply happen as a dynamic result of the rest of the system. "Emergence" comes from middle 17th century Latin in the sense of an "unforeseen occurrence." You can't plan for it or schedule it, but you can cultivate an environment where you can let it happen and benefit from it.

A classic example of emergence lies in the flocking behavior of birds. A computer simulation can use as few as three simple rules (along the lines of "don't run into each other") and suddenly you get very complex behavior as the flock wends and wafts its way gracefully through the sky, reforming around obstacles, and so on. None of this advanced behavior (such as reforming the same shape around an obstacle) is specified by the rules; it emerges from the dynamics of the system.

Simple rules, as with the birds simulation, lead to complex behavior. Complex rules, as with the tax law in most countries, lead to stupid behavior.

Many common software development practices have the unfortunate side-effect of eliminating any chance for emergent behavior. Most attempts at optimization – tying something down very explicitly – reduces the breadth and scope of interactions and relationships, which is the very source of emergence. In the flocking birds example, as with a well-designed system, it's the interactions and relationships that create the interesting behavior.

The harder we tighten things down, the less room there is for a creative, emergent solution. Whether it's locking down requirements before they are well understood or prematurely optimizing code, or inventing complex navigation and workflow scenarios before letting end users play with the system, the result is the same: an overly complicated, stupid system instead of a clean, elegant system that harnesses emergence.

Keep it small. Keep it simple. Let it happen.

–Andrew Hunt, The Pragmatic Programmers

The Three Musketeers

Use a team of three for version 1.0

For the first version of your app, start with only three
people. That's the magic number that will give you enough
manpower yet allow you to stay streamlined and agile.
Start with a developer, a designer, and a sweeper (someone
who can roam between both worlds).

Now sure, it's a challenge to build an app with only a
few people. But if you've got the right team, it's worth it.
Talented people don't need endless resources. They thrive
on the challenge of working within restraints and using
their creativity to solve problems. Your lack of manpower
means you'll be forced to deal with tradeoffs earlier in the
process – and that's alright. It will make you figure out
your priorities earlier rather than later. And you'll be able
to communicate without constantly having to worry about
leaving people out of the loop.

If you can't build your version one with three people, then
you either need different people or need to slim down
your initial version. Remember, it's OK to keep your first
version small and tight. You'll quickly get to see if your
idea has wings and, if it does, you'll have a clean, simple
base to build on.

Metcalfe's Law and project teams

Keep the team as small as possible. Metcalfe's Law, that "the value of a communication system grows at approximately the square of the number of users of the system," has a corollary when it comes to project teams: The efficiency of the team is approximately the inverse of the square of the number of members in the team. I'm beginning to think three people is optimal for a 1.0 product release...Start out by reducing the number of people you plan to add to the team, and then reduce some more.

–Marc Hedlund, entrepreneur-in-residence at O'Reilly Media

Communication flow

Communication flows more easily on small teams than large teams. If you're the only person on a project, communication is simple. The only communication path is between you and the customer. As the number of people on a project increases, however, so does the number of communication paths. It doesn't increase additively, as the number of people increases, it increases multiplicatively, proportional to the square of the number of people.

–Steve McConnell, Chief Software Engineer at Construx Software Builders Inc. (from Less is More: Jumpstarting Productivity with Small Teams)

Embrace Constraints

Let limitations guide you to creative solutions

There's never enough to go around. Not enough time. Not enough money. Not enough people.

That's a good thing.

Instead of freaking out about these constraints, embrace them. Let them guide you. Constraints drive innovation and force focus. Instead of trying to remove them, use them to your advantage.

When 37signals was building Basecamp, we had plenty of limitations. We had:

A design firm to run

Existing client work

A 7-hour time difference (David was doing the programming in Denmark, the rest of us were in the States)

A small team

No outside funding

We felt the "not enough" blues. So we kept our plate small. That way we could only put so much on it. We took big tasks and broke them up into small bits that we tackled one at a time. We moved step by step and prioritized as we went along.

That forced us to come up with creative solutions. We lowered our cost of change by always building less software. We gave people just enough features to solve their own problems their own way – and then we got out of the way. The time difference and distance between us made us more efficient in our communication. Instead of meeting in person, we communicated almost exclusively via IM and email which forced us to get to the point quickly.

Constraints are often advantages in disguise. Forget about venture capital, long release cycles, and quick hires. Instead, work with what you have.

Fight blight

What has been described as "creeping elegance" is probably better described as "feature blight," for like a fungus on a plant it gradually elaborates and blurs the true outline of the product while it drains its sap. The antidote to feature blight is, of course, the "constricting deadline." This results in features being discarded in proportion to the time it would take to implement them. It is often the case that the most useful features take the longest to implement. Thus the combination of the blight and the deadline yields software as we know and love it, comprised of bountiful quantities of useless features.

–Jef Raskin, author (from Why Software Is the Way It Is)

Be Yourself

Differentiate yourself from bigger companies by being personal and friendly

A lot of small companies make the mistake of trying to act big. It's as if they perceive their size as a weakness that needs to be covered up. Too bad. Being small can actually be a huge advantage, especially when it comes to communication.

Small companies enjoy fewer formalities, less bureaucracy, and more freedom. **Smaller companies are closer to the customer by default.** That means they can communicate in a more direct and personal way with customers. If you're small, you can use familiar language instead of jargon. Your site and your product can have a human voice instead of sounding like a corporate drone. Being small means you can talk *with* your customers, not down to them.

There are also advantages to internal communications at small companies too. You can ditch formalities. There's no need for arduous processes and multiple sign-offs on everything. Everyone in the process can speak openly and honestly. This unfettered flow of ideas is one of the big advantages of staying small.

Be proudly, defiantly truthful

Though you may think that a customer can be fooled by exaggerations on the number of staffers in your company or the breadth of your offerings, the smart ones, the ones you really want, will always learn the truth – whether through intuition or deduction. Embarrassingly, I've been a part of white lies like this in the past, and none of those situations ever resulted in what matters most to a business: meaningful, lasting and mutually beneficial relationships with people who had a real need for the services offered. The better course would have been to be proudly, defiantly truthful about the exact size and breadth of the company.

–Khoi Vinh, Subtraction.com and co-founder of Behavior LLC

Any time at all

No matter what business you are in, good customer service has got to be the biggest request that any client will ever make. We demand it for the services we use so why would we think our customers would be any different?

From the very beginning we made it easy and transparent for our customers to get in touch with us for any number or questions they might have. On our website we list a toll-free number that forwards to our mobile phones and on our business cards each of us list our mobile numbers. We emphasize to our customers that they can get in touch with us any time no matter what the problem might be. Our customers appreciate this level of trust and no one has ever abused this service.

–Edward Knittel, Director of Sales and Marketing, KennelSource

Priorities

What's the Big Idea

Explicitly define the one-point vision for your app

What does your app stand for? What's it really all about?

Before you start designing or coding anything you need to know the purpose of your product – the vision. Think big. Why does it exist? What makes it different than other similar products?

This vision will guide your decisions and keep you on a consistent path. Whenever there's a sticking point, ask, "Are we staying true to the vision?"

Your vision should be brief too. A sentence should be enough to get the idea across. Here's the vision for each of our products:

Basecamp: Project management is communication
Backpack: Bring life's loose ends together
Campfire: Group chat over IM sucks
Ta-da List: Competing with a post-it note
Writeboard: Word is overkill

With Basecamp, for example, the vision was "Project management is communication." We felt strongly that effective communication on a project leads to collective ownership, involvement, investment, and momentum. It gets everyone on the same page working toward a common goal. We knew if Basecamp could accomplish this, everything else would fall in line.

This vision led us to keep Basecamp as open and transparent as possible. Instead of limiting communication to within a firm, we gave clients access too. We thought less about permissions and more about encouraging all participants to take part. The vision is why we skipped charts, graphs, tables, reports, stats, and spreadsheets and instead focused on communication priorities like messages, comments, to-do lists, and sharing files.

Make the big decision about your vision upfront and all your future little decisions become much easier.

Whiteboard philosophy

Andy Hunt and I once wrote a debit card transaction switch. A major requirement was that the user of a debit card shouldn't have the same transaction applied to their account twice. In other words, no matter what sort of failure mode might happen, the error should be on the side of not processing a transaction rather than processing a duplicate transaction.

So, we wrote it on our shared whiteboard in big letters: Err in favor of users.

It joined about half-a-dozen other maxims. Jointly, these guided all those tricky decisions you make while building something complex. Together, these laws gave our application strong internal coherence and great external consistency.

-Dave Thomas, The Pragmatic Programmers

Make Mantra

Organizations need guideposts. They need an outline; employees need to know each day when they wake up why they're going to work. This outline should be short and sweet, and all encompassing: Why do you exist? What motivates you? I call this a mantra – a three- or four-word description of why you exist.

-Guy Kawasaki, author (from Make Mantra)

Ignore Details Early On

Work from large to small

We're crazy about details.

The space between objects
The perfect type leading
The perfect color
The perfect words
Four lines of code instead of seven
90% vs 89%
760px vs 750px
$39/month vs. $49/month

Success and satisfaction is in the details.

However, success isn't the only thing you'll find in the details. You'll also find stagnation, disagreement, meetings, and delays. These things can kill morale and lower your chances of success.

How often have you found yourself stuck on a single design or code element for a whole day? How often have you realized that the progress you made today wasn't real progress? This happens when you focus on details too early in the process. There's plenty of time to be a perfectionist. Just do it later.

Don't worry about the size of your headline font in week one. You don't need to nail that perfect shade of green in week two. You don't need to move that "submit" button three pixels to the right in week three. Just get the stuff on the page for now. Then use it. Make sure it works. Later on you can adjust and perfect it.

Details reveal themselves as you use what you're building. You'll see what needs more attention. You'll feel what's missing. You'll know which potholes to pave over because you'll keep hitting them. That's when you need to pay attention, not sooner.

The Devil's in the Details

I really got over the "get into details right away" attitude after I took some drawing classes...If you begin to draw the details right away you can be sure that the drawing is going to suck. In fact, you are completely missing the point.

You should begin by getting your proportions right for the whole scene. Then you sketch the largest objects in your scene, up to the smallest one. The sketch must be very loose up to this point.

Then you can proceed with shading which consists of bringing volume to life. You begin with only three tones (light, medium, dark). This gives you a tonal sketch. Then for each portion of your drawing you reevaluate three tonal shades and apply them. Do it until the volumes are there (requires multiple iteration)...

Work from large to small. Always.

-Patrick Lafleur, Creation Objet Inc. (from Signal vs. Noise)

It's a Problem When It's a Problem

Don't waste time on problems you don't have yet

Do you really need to worry about scaling to 100,000 customers today if it will take you two years to get there?

Do you really have to hire eight programmers if you only need three today?

Do you really need 12 top-of-the-line servers now if you can run on two for a year?

Just Wing It

People often spend too much time up front trying to solve problems they don't even have yet. Don't. Heck, we launched Basecamp without the ability to bill customers! Since the product billed in monthly cycles, we knew we had a 30-day gap to figure it out. We used that time to solve more urgent problems and then, after launch, we tackled billing. It worked out fine (and it forced us into a simple solution without unnecessary bells and whistles).

Don't sweat stuff until you actually must. Don't overbuild. Increase hardware and system software as necessary. If you're slow for a week or two it's not the end of the world. Just be honest: explain to your customers you're experiencing some growing pains. They may not be thrilled but they'll appreciate the candor.

Bottom Line: Make decisions just in time, when you have access to the real information you need. In the meanwhile, you'll be able to lavish attention on the things that require immediate care.

Hire the Right Customers

Find the core market for your application and focus solely on them

The customer is not always right. The truth is you have to sort out who's right and who's wrong for your app. The good news is that the internet makes finding the right people easier than ever.

If you try to please everyone, you won't please anyone

When we built Basecamp we focused our marketing on design firms. By narrowing our market this way, we made it more likely to attract passionate customers who, in turn, would evangelize the product. Know who your app is really intended for and focus on pleasing them.

The Best Call We Ever Made

The decision to aim Campaign Monitor strictly at the web design market was the best call we ever made. It allowed us to easily identify which features would be genuinely useful and, more importantly, which features to leave out. Not only have we attracted more customers by targeting a smaller group of people, these customers all have similar needs which makes our job much easier. There are loads of features in Campaign Monitor that would be useless to anyone but a web designer.

Focusing on a core market also makes it much easier to spread the word about your software. Now that we have a tightly defined audience, we can advertise where they frequent online, publish articles they might find interesting, and generally build a community around our product.

-David Greiner, founder, Campaign Monitor

Scale Later

You don't have a scaling problem yet

"Will my app scale when millions of people start using it?"

Ya know what? Wait until that actually happens. If you've got a huge number of people overloading your system then huzzah! That's one swell problem to have. The truth is the overwhelming majority of web apps are never going to reach that stage. And even if you do start to get overloaded it's usually not an all-or-nothing issue. You'll have time to adjust and respond to the problem. Plus, you'll have more real-world data and benchmarks after you launch which you can use to figure out the areas that need to be addressed.

For example, we ran Basecamp on a single server for the first year. Because we went with such a simple setup, it only took a week to implement. We didn't start with a cluster of 15 boxes or spend months worrying about scaling.

Did we experience any problems? A few. But we also realized that most of the problems we feared, like a brief slowdown, really weren't that big of a deal to customers. As long as you keep people in the loop, and are honest about the situation, they'll understand. In retrospect, we're quite glad we didn't delay launch for months in order to create "the perfect setup."

In the beginning, make building a solid core product your priority instead of obsessing over scalability and server farms. **Create a great app and then worry about what to do once it's wildly successful**. Otherwise you may waste energy, time, and money fixating on something that never even happens.

Believe it or not, the bigger problem isn't scaling, it's getting to the point where you have to scale. Without the first problem you won't have the second.

You have to revisit anyway

The fact is that everyone has scalability issues, no one can deal with their service going from zero to a few million users without revisiting almost every aspect of their design and architecture.

-Dare Obasanjo, Microsoft

Make Opinionated Software

Your app should take sides

Some people argue software should be agnostic. They say it's arrogant for developers to limit features or ignore feature requests. They say software should always be as flexible as possible.

We think that's bullshit. The best software has a vision. The best software takes sides. When someone uses software, they're not just looking for features, they're looking for an approach. They're looking for a vision. Decide what your vision is and run with it.

And remember, if they don't like your vision there are plenty of other visions out there for people. Don't go chasing people you'll never make happy.

A great example is the original wiki design. Ward Cunningham and friends deliberately stripped the wiki of many features that were considered integral to document collaboration in the past. Instead of attributing each change of the document to a certain person, they removed much of the visual representation of ownership. They made the content ego-less and time-less. They decided it wasn't important who wrote the content or when it was written. And that has made all the difference. This decision fostered a shared sense of community and was a key ingredient in the success of Wikipedia.

Our apps have followed a similar path. They don't try to be all things to all people. They have an attitude. They seek out customers who are actually partners. They speak to people who share our vision. You're either on the bus or off the bus.

Feature Selection

Half, Not Half-Assed

Build half a product, not a half-ass product

Beware of the "everything but the kitchen sink" approach to web app development. Throw in every decent idea that comes along and you'll just wind up with a half-assed version of your product. What you really want to do is build half a product that kicks ass.

Stick to what's truly essential. Good ideas can be tabled. **Take whatever you think your product should be and cut it in half**. Pare features down until you're left with only the most essential ones. Then do it again.

With Basecamp, we started with just the messages section. We knew that was the heart of the app so we ignored milestones, to-do lists, and other items for the time being. That let us base future decisions on real world usage instead of hunches.

Start off with a lean, smart app and let it gain traction. Then you can add to the solid foundation you've built.

It Just Doesn't Matter

Essentials only

Our favorite answer to the "why didn't you do this or why didn't you do that?" question is always: "Because it just doesn't matter." That statement embodies what makes a product great. Figuring out what matters and leaving out the rest.

When we launched Campfire we heard some of these questions from people checking out the product for the first time:

"Why time stamps only every 5 minutes? Why not time stamp every chat line?" Answer: It just doesn't matter. How often do you need to track a conversation by the second or even the minute? Certainly not 95% of the time. 5 minute stamps are sufficient because anything more specific just doesn't matter.

"Why don't you allow bold or italic or colored formatting in the chats?" Answer: It just doesn't matter. If you need to emphasize something use the trusty CAPS LOCK key or toss a few *'s around the word or phrase. Those solutions don't require additional software, tech support, processing power, or have a learning curve. Besides, heavy formatting in a simple text-based chat just doesn't matter.

"Why don't you show the total number of people in the room at a given time?" Answer: It just doesn't matter. Everyone's name is listed so you know who's there, but what difference does it make if there's 12 or 16 people? If it doesn't change your behavior, then it just doesn't matter.

Would these things be nice to have? Sure. But are they essential? Do they really matter? Nope. And that's why we left them out.

The best designers and the best programmers aren't the ones with the best skills, or the nimblest fingers, or the ones who can rock and roll with Photoshop or their environment of choice, they are the ones that can determine what just doesn't matter. That's where the real gains are made.

Most of the time you spend is wasted on things that just don't matter. If you can cut out the work and thinking that just don't matter, you'll achieve productivity you've never imagined.

Start With No

Make features work hard to be implemented

The secret to building half a product instead of a half-ass product is saying no.

Each time you say yes to a feature, you're adopting a child. You have to take your baby through a whole chain of events (e.g. design, implementation, testing, etc.). And once that feature's out there, you're stuck with it. Just try to take a released feature away from customers and see how pissed off they get.

Don't be a yes-man

Make each feature work hard to be implemented. Make each feature prove itself and show that it's a survivor. It's like "Fight Club." You should only consider features if they're willing to stand on the porch for three days waiting to be let in.

That's why you start with no. Every new feature request that comes to us – or from us – meets a no. We listen but don't act. The initial response is "not now." If a request for a feature keeps coming back, that's when we know it's time to take a deeper look. Then, and only then, do we start considering the feature for real.

And what do you say to people who complain when you won't adopt their feature idea? Remind them why they like the app in the first place. "You like it because we say no. You like it because it doesn't do 100 other things. You like it because it doesn't try to please everyone all the time."

"We Don't Want a Thousand Features"

Steve Jobs gave a small private presentation about the iTunes Music Store to some independent record label people. My favorite line of the day was when people kept raising their hand saying, "Does it do [x]?", "Do you plan to add [y]?". Finally Jobs said, "Wait wait – put your hands down. Listen: I know you have a thousand ideas for all the cool features iTunes could have. So do we. But we don't want a thousand features. That would be ugly. Innovation is not about saying yes to everything. It's about saying NO to all but the most crucial features."

-Derek Sivers, president and programmer, CD Baby
and HostBaby (from Say NO by default)

Hidden Costs

Expose the price of new features

Even if a feature makes it past the "no" stage, you still need to expose its hidden costs.

For example, be on the lookout for feature loops (i.e. features that lead to more features). We've had requests to add a meetings tab to Basecamp. Seems simple enough until you examine it closely. Think of all the different items a meetings tab might require: location, time, room, people, email invites, calendar integration, support documentation, etc. That's not to mention that we'd have to change promotional screenshots, tour pages, FAQ/help pages, the terms of service, and more. Before you know it, a simple idea can snowball into a major headache.

For every new feature you need to...

1. Say no.
2. Force the feature to prove its value.
3. If "no" again, end here. If "yes," continue...
4. Sketch the screen(s)/UI.
5. Design the screen(s)/UI.
6. Code it.
7-15. Test, tweak, test, tweak, test, tweak, test, tweak...
16. Check to see if help text needs to be modified.
17. Update the product tour (if necessary).
18. Update the marketing copy (if necessary).
19. Update the terms of service (if necessary).
20. Check to see if any promises were broken.
21. Check to see if pricing structure is affected.
22. Launch.

Can You Handle It?

Build something you can manage

If you launch an affiliate program do you have the systems in place to handle the accounting and payouts? Maybe you should just let people earn credit against their membership fees instead of writing, signing, and mailing a check each month.

Can you afford to give away 1 GB of space for free just because Google does? Maybe you should start small at 100 MB, or only provide space on paying accounts.

Bottom line: Build products and offer services you can manage. It's easy to make promises. It's much harder to keep them. Make sure whatever it is that you're doing is something you can actually sustain – organizationally, strategically, and financially.

Human Solutions

Build software for general concepts and encourage people to create their own solutions

Don't force conventions on people. Instead make your software general so everyone can find their own solution. Give people just enough to solve their own problems their own way. And then get out of the way.

When we built Ta-da List we intentionally omitted a lot of stuff. There's no way to assign a to-do to someone, there's no way to mark a date due, there's no way to categorize items, etc.

We kept the tool clean and uncluttered by letting people get creative. People figured out how to solve issues on their own. If they wanted to add a date to a to-do item they could just add (due: April 7, 2006) to the front of the item. If they wanted to add a category, they could just add [Books] to the front of the item. Ideal? No. Infinitely flexible? Yes.

If we tried to build software to specifically handle these scenarios, we'd be making it less useful for all the cases when those concerns don't apply.

Do the best job you can with the root of the problem then step aside. People will find their own solutions and conventions within your general framework.

Forget Feature Requests

Let your customers remind you what's important

Customers want everything under the sun. They'll avalanche you with feature requests. Just check out our product forums; The feature request category always trumps the others by a wide margin.

We'll hear about "this little extra feature" or "this can't be hard" or "wouldn't it be easy to add this" or "it should take just a few seconds to put it in" or "if you added this I'd pay twice as much" and so on.

Of course we don't fault people for making requests. We encourage it and we want to hear what they have to say. Most everything we add to our products starts out as a customer request.

But, as we mentioned before, your first response should be a no. So what do you do with all these requests that pour in? Where do you store them? **How do you manage them? You don't. Just read them and then throw them away.**

Yup, read them, throw them away, and forget them. It sounds blasphemous but the ones that are important will keep bubbling up anyway. Those are the only ones you need to remember. Those are the truly essential ones. Don't worry about tracking and saving each request that comes in. Let your customers be your memory. If it's really worth remembering, they'll remind you until you can't forget.

How did we come to this conclusion? When we first launched Basecamp we tracked every major feature request on a Basecamp to-do list. When a request was repeated by someone else we'd update the list with an extra hash mark (II or III or IIII, etc). We figured that one day we'd review this list and start working from the most requested features on down.

But the truth is we never looked at it again. We already knew what needed to be done next because our customers constantly reminded us by making the same requests over and over again. There was no need for a list or lots of analysis because it was all happening in real time. You can't forget what's important when you are reminded of it every day.

And one more thing: Just because x number of people request something, doesn't mean you *have* to include it. Sometimes it's better to just say no and maintain your vision for the product.

Hold the Mayo

Ask people what they *don't* want

Most software surveys and research questions are centered around what people want in a product. "What feature do you think is missing?" "If you could add just one thing, what would it be?" "What would make this product more useful for you?"

What about the other side of the coin? Why not ask people what they don't want? "If you could remove one feature, what would it be?" "What don't you use?" "What gets in your way the most?"

More isn't the answer. Sometimes the biggest favor you can do for customers is to leave something out.

Innovation Comes From Saying No

[Innovation] comes from saying no to 1,000 things to make sure we don't get on the wrong track or try to do too much. We're always thinking about new markets we could enter, but it's only by saying no that you can concentrate on the things that are really important.

-Steve Jobs, CEO, Apple (from The Seed of Apple's Innovation)

Process

Race to Running Software

Get something real up and running quickly

Running software is the best way to build momentum, rally your team, and flush out ideas that don't work. It should be your number one priority from day one.

It's OK to do less, skip details, and take shortcuts in your process if it'll lead to running software faster. Once you're there, you'll be rewarded with a significantly more accurate perspective on how to proceed. Stories, wireframes, even HTML mockups, are just approximations. Running software is real.

With real, running software everyone gets closer to true understanding and agreement. You avoid heated arguments over sketches and paragraphs that wind up turning out not to matter anyway. You realize that parts you thought were trivial are actually quite crucial.

Real things lead to real reactions. And that's how you get to the truth.

....

The Real Thing Leads to Agreement

When a group of different people set out to try and find out what is harmonious...their opinions about it will tend to converge if they are mocking up full-scale, real stuff. Of course, if they're making sketches or throwing out ideas, they won't agree. But, if you start making the real thing, one tends to reach agreement.

-Christopher Alexander, Emeritus Professor of Architecture at the University of California, Berkeley (from Contrasting Concepts of Harmony in Architecture)

Get It Working ASAP

I do not think I've ever been involved with a software project
– large or small – that was successful in terms of schedule, cost,
or functionality that started with a long period of planning
and discussion and no concurrent development. It is simply
too easy, and sometimes fun, to waste valuable time inventing
features that turn out to be unnecessary or unimplementable.

This applies at all levels of development and "get something real
up and running" is a fractal mantra. It doesn't just apply to the
project as a whole, it is at least equally applicable to the smaller-scale
development of components from which the application is built.

When there is a working implementation of a key component
available, developers want to understand how it will or won't
work with their piece of the application and will generally try to
use it as soon as they can. Even if the implementation isn't perfect
or complete at first, this early collaboration usually leads to well-
defined interfaces and features that do exactly what they need to.

-Matt Hamer, developer and product manager, Kinja

Rinse and Repeat

Work in iterations

Don't expect to get it right the first time. Let the app grow and speak to you. Let it morph and evolve. With web-based software there's no need to ship perfection. Design screens, use them, analyze them, and then start over again.

Instead of banking on getting everything right upfront, the iterative process lets you continue to make informed deci-sions as you go along. Plus, you'll get an active app up and running quicker since you're not striving for perfection right out the gate. The result is real feedback and real guid-ance on what requires your attention.

Iterations lead to liberation

You don't need to aim for perfection on the first try if you know it's just going to be done again later anyway. Knowing that you're going to revisit issues is a great moti-vator to just get ideas out there to see if they'll fly.

Maybe you're smarter than me

Maybe you're a LOT smarter than me.

It's entirely possible. In fact, it's likely. However, if you're like most people, then like me, you have trouble imagining what you can't see and feel and touch.

Human beings are extremely good at responding to things in the environment. We know how to panic when a tiger enters the room, and how to clean up after a devastating flood. Unfortunately, we're terrible at planning ahead, at understanding the ramifications of our actions and in prioritizing the stuff that really matters.

Perhaps you are one of the few individuals who can keep it all in your head. It doesn't really matter.

Web 2.0, the world where we start by assuming that everyone already uses the web, allows smart developers to put this human frailty to work for them. How? By allowing your users to tell you what they think while there's still time to do something about it.

And that last sentence explains why you should develop this way and how you might want to promote/launch.

Get your story straight. Make sure the pieces work. Then launch and revise.

No one is as smart as all of us.

-Seth Godin, author/entrepreneur

From Idea to Implementation

Go from brainstorm to sketches to HTML to coding

Here's the process we use to Get Real:

Brainstorm

Come up with ideas. What is this product going to do? For Basecamp, we looked at our own needs. We wanted to post project updates. We wanted clients to participate. We knew that projects had milestones. We wanted to centralize archives so people could easily review old stuff. We wanted to have a big-picture, bird's-eye view of what's going on with all our projects. Together, those assumptions, and a few others, served as our foundation.

This stage is not about nitty gritty details. This is about big questions. What does the app need to do? How will we know when it's useful? What exactly are we going to make? This is about high level ideas, not pixel-level discussions. At this stage, those kinds of details just aren't meaningful.

Paper sketches

Sketches are quick, dirty, and cheap and that's exactly how you want to start out. Draw stuff. Scrawl stuff. Boxes, circles, lines. Get your ideas out of your head and onto paper. The goal at this point should be to convert concepts into rough interface designs. This step is all about experimentation. There are no wrong answers.

Create HTML screens

Make an HTML version of that feature (or section or flow, if it's more appropriate). Get something real posted so everyone can see what it looks like on screen.

For Basecamp, we first did the "post a message" screen, then the "edit a message" screen, and it went on from there.

Don't write any programming code yet. Just build a mock-up in HTML and CSS. Implementation comes later.

Code it

When the mock-up looks good and demonstrates enough of the necessary functionality, go ahead and plug in the programming code.

During this whole process remember to stay flexible and expect multiple iterations. You should feel free to throw away the deliverable of any particular step and start again if it turns out crappy. It's natural to go through this cycle multiple times.

Avoid Preferences

Decide the little details so your customers don't have to

You're faced with a tough decision: how many messages do we include on each page? Your first inclination may be to say, "Let's just make it a preference where people can choose 25, 50, or 100." That's the easy way out though. Just make a decision.

Preferences are a way to avoid making tough decisions

Instead of using your expertise to choose the best path, you're leaving it in the hands of customers. It may seem like you're doing them a favor but you're just making busy work for them (and it's likely they're busy enough). For customers, preference screens with an endless amount of options are a headache, not a blessing. Customers shouldn't have to think about every nitty gritty detail – don't put that burden on them when it should be your responsibility.

Preferences are also evil because they create more software. More options require more code. And there's all the extra testing and designing you need to do too. You'll also wind up with preference permutations and interface screens that you never even see. That means bugs that you don't know about: broken layouts, busted tables, strange pagination issues, etc.

Make the call

Make simple decisions on behalf of your customers. That's what we did in Basecamp. The number of messages per page is 25. On the overview page, the last 25 items are shown. Messages are sorted in reverse chronological order. The five most recent projects are shown in the dashboard. There aren't any options. That's just the way it is.

Yes, you might make a bad call. But so what. If you do, people will complain and tell you about it. As always, you can adjust. Getting Real is all about being able to change on the fly.

Preferences Have a Cost

It turns out that preferences have a cost. Of course, some preferences also have important benefits – and can be crucial interface features. But each one has a price, and you have to carefully consider its value. Many users and developers don't understand this, and end up with a lot of cost and little value for their preferences dollar...I find that if you're hard-core disciplined about having good defaults that Just Work instead of lazily adding preferences, that naturally leads the overall UI in the right direction.

-Havoc Pennington, tech lead, Red Hat (from Free software and good user interfaces)

"Done!"

Decisions are temporary so make the call and move on

Done. Start to think of it as a magical word. When you get to done it means something's been accomplished. A decision has been made and you can move on. Done means you're building momentum.

But wait, what if you screw up and make the wrong call? It's OK. **This isn't brain surgery, it's a web app**. As we keep saying, you'll likely have to revisit features and ideas multiple times during the process anyway. No matter how much you plan you're likely to get half wrong anyway. So don't do the "paralyis through analysis" thing. That only slows progress and saps morale.

Instead, value the importance of moving on and moving forward. Get in the rhythm of making decisions. Make a quick, simple call and then go back and change that decision if it doesn't work out.

Accept that decisions are temporary. Accept that mistakes will happen and realize it's no big deal as long as you can correct them quickly. Execute, build momentum, and move on.

Be An Executioner

It's so funny when I hear people being so protective of ideas. (People who want me to sign an NDA to tell me the simplest idea.)

To me, ideas are worth nothing unless executed. They are just a multiplier. Execution is worth millions.

Explanation:

Awful idea = -1
Weak idea = 1
So-so idea = 5
Good idea = 10
Great idea = 15
Brilliant idea = 20

No execution = $1
Weak execution = $1000
So-so execution = $10,000
Good execution = $100,000
Great execution = $1,000,000
Brilliant execution = $10,000,000

To make a business, you need to multiply the two.

The most brilliant idea, with no execution, is worth $20. The most brilliant idea takes great execution to be worth $20,000,000.

That's why I don't want to hear people's ideas. I'm not interested until I see their execution.

-Derek Sivers, president and programmer, CD Baby and HostBaby

Test in the Wild

Test your app via real world usage

There's no substitute for real people using your app in real ways. Get real data. Get real feedback. Then improve based on that info.

Formal usability testing is too stiff. Lab settings don't reflect reality. If you stand over someone's shoulder, you'll get some idea of what's working or not but people generally don't perform well in front of a camera. When someone else is watching, people are especially careful not to make mistakes – yet mistakes are exactly what you're looking for.

Instead, release beta features to a select few inside the real application itself. Have them use the beta features alongside the released features. This will expose these features to people's real data and real workflow. And that's where you'll get real results.

Further, don't have a release version and a beta version. They should always be the same thing. A separate beta version will only get a superficial walk through. The real version, with some beta features sprinkled in, will get the full workout.

The Beta Book

If developers are nervous releasing code, then publishers and authors are terrified of releasing books. Once a book gets committed to paper, it's seen as a big hairy deal to change it. (It really isn't, but perception and memories of problems with old technologies still linger in the industry.) So, publishers go to a lot of trouble (and expense) to try to make books "right" before they're released.

When I wrote the book Agile Web Development With Rails, there was a lot of pent up demand among developers: give us the book now – we want to learn about Rails. But I'd fallen into the mindset of a publisher. "It isn't ready yet," I'd say. But pressure from the community and some egging on from David Heinemeier Hansson changed my mind. We released the book in PDF form about 2 months before it was complete. The results were spectacular. Not only did we sell a lot of books, but we got feedback – a lot of feedback. I set up an automated system to capture readers' comments, and in the end got almost 850 reports or typos, technical errors, and suggestions for new content. Almost all made their way into the final book.

It was a win-win: I got to deliver a much improved paper book, and the community got early access to something they wanted. And if you're in a competitive race, getting something out earlier helps folks commit to you and not your competition.

-Dave Thomas, The Pragmatic Programmers

Do it quick

1. Decide if it's worth doing, and if so:
2. Do it quick – not perfect. just do it.
3. Save it. upload it. publish it
4. See what people think

Though I'm always reluctant to add new features to things, once I have that "yeah!" moment of deciding something is worth doing, it's usually up on the website a few hours later, flawed but launched, letting feedback guide future refinement of it.

-Derek Sivers, president and programmer, CD Baby and HostBaby

Shrink Your Time

Break it down

Estimates that stretch into weeks or months are fantasies.
The truth is you just don't know what's going to happen
that far in advance.

So shrink your time. Keep breaking down timeframes into
smaller chunks. Instead of a 12 week project, think of it as
12 weeklong projects. Instead of guesstimating at tasks that
take 30+ hours, break them down into more realistic 6-10
hour chunks. Then proceed one step at a time.

The same theory applies to other problems too. Are you
facing an issue that's too big to wrap your mind around?
Break it down. Keep dividing problems into smaller and
smaller pieces until you're able to digest them.

Smaller Tasks and Smaller Timelines

Software developers are a special breed of optimist:
when presented with a programming task, they think,
"That'll be easy! Won't take much time at all."

So, give a programmer three weeks to complete a large task, and she'll
spend two and a half procrastinating, and then one programming. The
off-schedule result will probably meet the wrong requirements, because
the task turned out to be more complex than it seemed. Plus, who can
remember what the team agreed upon three weeks ago?

Give a programmer an afternoon to code a small, specific module and
she'll crank it out, ready to move onto the next one.

Smaller tasks and smaller timelines are more manageable, hide
fewer possible requirement misunderstandings, and cost less to
change your mind about or re-do. Smaller timelines keep developers
engaged and give them more opportunities to enjoy a sense of
accomplishment and less reason to think, "Oh I've got plenty of time
to do that. For now, let me finish rating songs in my iTunes library."

-Gina Trapani, web developer and editor of Lifehacker,
the productivity and software guide

True Factors

Next time someone tries to pin you down for an exact answer to an
unknowable question – whether it's for a deadline date, a final project
cost, or the volume of milk that would fit in the Grand Canyon – just
start by taking the air out of the room: say "I don't know."

Far from damaging your credibility, this demonstrates the care you
bring to your decision-making. You're not going to just say words
to sound smart. It also levels the playing field by reframing the
question as a collaborative conversation. By learning how exact your
estimate needs to be (and why), you can work together to develop a
shared understanding about the true factors behind the numbers.

-Merlin Mann, creator and editor of 43folders.com

Solve The One Problem Staring You in the Face

My absolute favorite thing to happen on the web in recent memory is the release and adoption of the "nofollow" attribute. Nobody talked about it beforehand. There were no conferences or committees where a bunch of yahoos could debate its semantic or grammatical nature. No RFC that could turn a simple idea into a 20-line XML snippet I'd have to read up on just to figure out how to use, and then not use because I wasn't sure if I was formatting for version .3 or 3.3b.

It's simple, it's effective, it provided an option for people who wanted an option – and that is far more important when dealing with a population of the web that doesn't care about specifications or deference.

Sometimes solving the next twenty problems is not as useful or as prudent as solving the one staring us right in the face. It wasn't just a small victory against spam (all victories against spam are small), but a victory for those of us who enjoy the simple and swift results that being a web developer is all about.

-Andre Torrez, programmer and VP of Engineering
at Federated Media Publishing

The Organization

Unity

Don't split into silos

Too many companies separate design, development, copy-writing, support, and marketing into different silos. While specialization has its advantages, it also creates a situation where staffers see just their own little world instead of the entire context of the web app.

As much as possible, integrate your team so there's a healthy back-and-forth dialogue throughout the process. Set up a system of checks and balances. Don't let things get lost in translation. Have copywriters work with designers. Make sure support queries are seen by developers.

Even better, hire people with multiple talents who can wear different hats during development. The end result will be a more harmonious product.

Alone Time

People need uninterrupted time to get things done

37signals is spread out over four cities and eight time zones. From Provo, Utah to Copenhagen, Denmark, the five of us are eight hours apart. One *positive* side effect of this eight hour difference is alone time.

There are only about 4-5 hours during the day that we're all up and working together. At other times, the US team is sleeping while David, who's in Denmark, is working. The rest of the time, we're working while David is sleeping. This gives us about half of the day together and the other half alone.

Guess which part of the day we get the most work done? The alone part. It's not that surprising really. Many people prefer to work either early in the morning or late at night – times when they're not being bothered.

When you have a long stretch when you aren't bothered, you can get in the zone. The zone is when you are most productive. It's when you don't have to mindshift between various tasks. It's when you aren't interrupted to answer a question or look up something or send an email or answer an IM. The alone zone is where real progress is made.

Getting in the zone takes time. And that's why interruption is your enemy. It's like REM sleep – you don't just go to REM sleep, you go to sleep first and you make your way to REM. Any interruptions force you to start over. REM is where the real sleep magic happens. **The alone time zone is where the real development magic happens**.
Set up a rule at work: Make half the day alone time. From 10am-2pm, no one can talk to one another (except during lunch). Or make the first or the last half of the day the alone time period. Just make sure this period is contiguous in order to avoid productivity-killing interruptions.

A successful alone time period means letting go of communication addiction. During alone time, give up instant messaging, phone calls, and meetings. Avoid any email thread that's going to require an immediate response. Just shut up and get to work.

Get Into the Groove

We all know that knowledge workers work best by getting into "flow", also known as being "in the zone", where they are fully concentrated on their work and fully tuned out of their environment. They lose track of time and produce great stuff through absolute concentration... trouble is that it's so easy to get knocked out of the zone. Noise, phone calls, going out for lunch, having to drive 5 minutes to Starbucks for coffee, and interruptions by coworkers – especially interruptions by coworkers – all knock you out of the zone. If you take a 1 minute interruption by a coworker asking you a question, and this knocks out your concentration enough that it takes you half an hour to get productive again, your overall productivity is in serious trouble.

-Joel Spolsky, software developer, Fog Creek Software
(from Where do These People Get Their (Unoriginal) Ideas?)

Meetings Are Toxic

Don't have meetings

Do you really need a meeting? Meetings usually arise when a concept isn't clear enough. Instead of resorting to a meeting, try to simplify the concept so you can discuss it quickly via email or IM or Campfire. The goal is to avoid meetings. Every minute you avoid spending in a meeting is a minute you can get real work done instead.

There's nothing more toxic to productivity than a meeting. Here's a few reasons why:

They break your work day into small, incoherent pieces that disrupt your natural workflow

They're usually about words and abstract concepts, not real things (like a piece of code or some interface design)

They usually convey an abysmally small amount of information per minute

They often contain at least one moron that inevitably gets his turn to waste everyone's time with nonsense

They drift off-subject easier than a Chicago cab in heavy snow

They frequently have agendas so vague nobody is really sure what they are about

They require thorough preparation that people rarely do anyway

For those times when you *absolutely must* have a meeting (this should be a rare event), stick to these simple rules:

Set a 30 minute timer. When it rings, meeting's over. Period.

Invite as few people as possible.

Never have a meeting without a clear agenda.

Have fewer meetings

There are too many meetings. Push back on meetings that do not make sense or are unproductive. Only book a meeting when you have an important business issue to discuss and you want or need input, approval, or agreement. Even then, resist the urge to invite everyone and their brother – don't waste people's time unnecessarily.

-Lisa Haneberg, author (from Don't Let Meetings Rule!)

Break it Down

As projects grow, adding people has a diminishing return. One of the most interesting reasons is the increased number of communications channels. Two people can only talk to each other; there's only a single comm path. Three workers have three communications paths; 4 have 6. In fact, the growth of links is exponential... Pretty soon memos and meetings eat up the entire work day.

The solution is clear: break teams into smaller, autonomous and independent units to reduce these communications links.

Similarly, cut programs into smaller units. Since a large part of the problem stems from dependencies (global variables, data passed between functions, shared hardware, etc.), find a way to partition the program to eliminate – or minimize – the dependencies between units.

-The Ganssle Group (from Keep It Small)

Seek and Celebrate Small Victories

Release something today

The most important thing in software development is motivation. Motivation is local – if you aren't motivated by what you are working on right now, then chances are it won't be as good as it should be. In fact, it's probably going to suck.

Long, drawn out release cycles are motivation killers. They insert too much time between celebrations. On the other hand, quick wins that you can celebrate are great motivators. If you let lengthy release cycles quash quick wins, you kill the motivation. And that can kill your product.

So, if you're in the middle of a months-long release cycle, dedicate a day a week (or every two weeks) for some small victories. Ask yourself "What can we do and release in 4 hours?" And then do it. It could be...

A new simple feature

A small enhancement to an existing feature

Rewriting some help text to reduce the support burden

Removing some form fields that you really don't need

When you find those 4-hour quick wins, you'll find celebration. That builds morale, increases motivation, and reaffirms that the team is headed in the right direction.

Staffing

Hire Less and Hire Later

Add slow to go fast

There's no need to get big early – or later. Even if you have access to 100 of the very best people, it's still a bad idea to try and hire them all at once. There's no way that you can immediately assimilate that many people into a coherent culture. You'll have training headaches, personality clashes, communication lapses, people going in different directions, and more.

So don't hire. Really. Don't hire people. Look for another way. Is the work that's burdening you really necessary? What if you just don't do it? Can you solve the problem with a slice of software or a change of practice instead?

Whenever Jack Welch, former CEO of GE, used to fire someone, he didn't immediately hire a replacement. He wanted to see how long GE could get along *without that person and that position*. We're certainly not advocating firing people to test this theory, but we do think Jack is on to something: You don't need as many people as you think.

If there's no other way, then consider a hire. But you should know exactly who to get, how to introduce them to the work, and the exact pain you expect them to relieve.

Brooks' law

Adding people to a late software project makes it later.

-*Fred Brooks*

Programming and Mozart's Requiem

A single good programmer working on a single task has no coordination or communication overhead. Five programmers working on the same task must coordinate and communicate. That takes a lot of time...

The real trouble with using a lot of mediocre programmers instead of a couple of good ones is that no matter how long they work, they never produce something as good as what the great programmers can produce.

Five Antonio Salieris won't produce Mozart's Requiem. Ever. Not if they work for 100 years.

-Joel Spolsky, software developer, Fog Creek Software
(from Hitting the High Notes)

Kick the Tires

Work with prospective employees on a test-basis first

It's one thing to look at a portfolio, resume, code example, or previous work. It's another thing to actually work with someone. Whenever possible, take potential new team members out for a "test drive."

Before we hire anyone we give them a small project to chew on first. We see how they handle the project, how they communicate, how they work, etc. Working with someone as they design or code a few screens will give you a ton of insight. You'll learn pretty quickly whether or not the right vibe is there.

Scheduling can be tough for this sort of thing but even if it's for just 20 or 40 hours, it's better than nothing. If it's a good or bad fit, it will be obvious. And if not, both sides save themselves a lot of trouble and risk by testing out the situation first.

Start small

Try a small test assignment to start. Don't leap in with all of your work at once. Give your new [virtual assistant] a test project or two to work on and see how the chemistry develops. In the beginning, it's too easy to gloss over potential problems with rose-colored glasses. Make it clear this is a test run.

> *-Suzanne Falter-Barns, author/creativity expert (from*
> *How To Find And Keep The Perfect VA)*

Actions, Not Words

Judge potential tech hires on open source contributions

The typical method of hiring for technical positions
– based on degrees, resumés, etc. – is silly in a lot of ways.
Does it really matter where someone's degree is from or
their GPA? Can you really trust a resumé or a reference?

Open source is a gift to those who need to hire technical
people. With open source, you can track someone's work
and contributions – good and bad – over a lengthy period
of time.

That means you can judge people by their actions instead
of just their words. You can make a decision based on the
things that really matter:

Quality of work
Many programmers can talk the talk but trip
when it comes time to walk the walk. With open
source, you get the nitty-gritty specifics of a
person's programming skills and practices.

Cultural perspective
Programing is all about decisions. Lots and lots of
them. Decisions are guided by your cultural vantage
point, values, and ideals. Look at the specific decisions
made by a candidate in coding, testing, and community
arguments to see whether you've got a cultural match.
If there's no fit here, each decision will be a struggle.

Level of passion
By definition, involvement in open source requires

at least some passion. Otherwise why would this person spend free time sitting in front of a screen? The amount of open source involvement often shows how much a candidate truly cares about programming.

Completion percentage
All the smarts, proper cultural leanings, and passion don't amount to valuable software if a person can't get stuff done. Unfortunately, lots of programmers can't. So look for that zeal to ship. Hire someone who needs to get it out the door and is willing to make the pragmatic trade-offs this may require.

Social match
Working with someone over a long period of time, during both stress/relaxation and highs/lows, will show you their real personality. If someone's lacking in manners or social skills, filter them out.

When it comes to programmers, we only hire people we know through open source. We think doing anything else is irresponsible. We hired Jamis because we followed his releases and participation in the Ruby community. He excelled in all the areas mentioned above. It wasn't necessary to rely on secondary factors since we could judge him based on what really matters: the quality of his work.

And don't worry that extra-curricular activities will take focus and passion away from a staffer's day job. It's like the old cliché says: If you want something done, ask the busiest person you know. Jamis and David are two of the heaviest contributors to Rails and still manage to drive 37signals technically. People who love to program and get things done are exactly the kind of people you want on your team.

Open Source Passion

What you want the most from a new hire is passion for
what he does, and there's no better way of showing it
than a trace of commitment in open source projects.

*-Jarkko Laine, software developer (from Loudthinking.com:
Reduce the risk, hire from open source)*

Get Well Rounded Individuals

Go for quick learning generalists over ingrained specialists

We'll never hire someone who's an information architect. It's just too overly specific. With a small team like ours, it doesn't make sense to hire people with such a narrowly defined skill-set.

Small teams need people who can wear different hats. You need designers who can write. You need programmers who understand design. Everyone should have an idea about how to architect information (whatever that may mean). Everyone needs to have an organized mind. Everyone needs to be able to communicate with customers.

And everyone needs to be willing and able to shift gears down the road. Keep in mind that small teams often need to change direction and do it quickly. You want someone who can adjust and learn and flow as opposed to a stick-in-the-mud who can do only one thing.

You Can't Fake Enthusiasm

Go for happy and average over frustrated and great

Enthusiasm. It's one attribute you just can't fake. When it comes time to hire, don't think you need a guru or a tech-celebrity. Often, they're just primadonnas anyway. A happy yet average employee is better than a disgruntled expert.

Find someone who's enthusiastic. Someone you can trust to get things done when left alone. Someone who's suffered at a bigger, slower company and longs for a new environment. Someone who's excited to build what you're building. Someone who hates the same things you hate. Someone who's thrilled to climb aboard your train.

Extra points for asking questions

Observe whether a potential hire asks a lot of questions about your project. Passionate programmers want to understand a problem as well as possible and will quickly propose potential solutions and improvements, which leads to a lot of questions. Clarifying questions also reveal an understanding that your project could be implemented thousands of different ways and it's essential to nail down as explicitly as possible exactly how you imagine your web app working. As you dig into the details, you'll develop a sense of whether the person is a good cultural match.

-Eric Stephens, BuildV1.com

Wordsmiths

Hire good writers

If you are trying to decide between a few people to fill a position, always hire the better writer. It doesn't matter if that person is a designer, programmer, marketer, salesperson, or whatever, the writing skills will pay off. Effective, concise writing and editing leads to effective, concise code, design, emails, instant messages, and more.

That's because being a good writer is about more than words. Good writers know how to communicate. They make things easy to understand. They can put themselves in someone else's shoes. They know what to omit. They think clearly. And those are the qualities you need.

An Organized Mind

Good writing skills are an indicator of an organized mind which is capable of arranging information and argument in a systematic fashion and also helping (not making) other people understand things. It spills over into code, personal communications, instant messaging (for those long-distance collaborations), and even such esoteric concepts as professionalism and reliability.

-Dustin J. Mitchell, developer

Clear Writing Leads To Clear Thinking

Clear writing leads to clear thinking. You don't know what you know until you try to express it. Good writing is partly a matter of character. Instead of doing what's easy for you, do what's easy for your reader.

-Michael A. Covington, Professor of Computer Science
The University of Georgia

Interface Design

Interface First

Design the interface before you start programming

Too many apps start with a program-first mentality. That's a bad idea. Programming is the heaviest component of building an app, meaning it's the most expensive and hardest to change. Instead, start by designing first.

Design is relatively light. A paper sketch is cheap and easy to change. HTML designs are still relatively simple to modify (or throw out). That's not true of programming. Designing first keeps you flexible. Programming first fences you in and sets you up for additional costs.

Another reason to design first is that **the interface is your product**. What people see is what you're selling. If you just slap an interface on at the end, the gaps will show.

We start with the interface so we can see how the app looks and feels from the beginning. It's constantly being revised throughout the process. Does it make sense? Is it easy to use? Does it solve the problem at hand? These are questions you can only truly answer when you're dealing with real screens. Designing first keeps you flexible and gets you to those answers sooner in the process rather than later.

The Orange Pen That Started Blinksale

As soon as I realized my frustration with off-the-shelf invoicing software, I decided to draw out how I would prefer my invoicing solution to work. I pulled out an orange pen, because it was the only thing handy that evening, and had about 75 percent of the UI drawn out within a few hours. I showed it to my wife, Rachel, who was ironing at the time, and asked, "What do you think?" And she replied with a smile, "You need to do this. For real."

Over the next two weeks I refined the designs, and completely mocked-up static HTML pages for almost the entire first version of what would become Blinksale. We never did any wireframes beyond those orange-pen sketches, and getting straight into the HTML design helped us stay excited about how "real" the project was becoming, even though at the time we really didn't know what we were getting into.

Once the HTML mockups were completed, we approached our developer, Scott, with the idea for Blinksale. Having most of the UI designed up front was extremely beneficial on several levels. First, it gave Scott a real vision and excitement for where we were going. It was much more than just an idea, it was real. Second, it helped us accurately gauge how much of Scott's effort and time it would require to turn the design into a functioning application. When you're financially bootstrapping a project, the earlier you can predict budget requirements, the better. The UI design became our benchmark for the initial project scope. Finally, the UI design served as a guide to remind us what the application was about as we progressed further into development. As we were tempted to add new features, we couldn't simply say, "Sure, let's add that!" We had to go back to the design and ask ourselves where that new feature would go, and if it didn't have a place, it wouldn't get added.

-Josh Williams, founder, Blinksale

Epicenter Design

Start from the core of the page and build outward

Epicenter design focuses on the true essence of the page – the epicenter – and then builds outward. This means that, at the start, you ignore the extremities: the navigation/tabs, footer, colors, sidebar, logo, etc. Instead, you start at the epicenter and design the most important piece of content first.

Whatever the page absolutely can't live without is the epicenter. For example, if you're designing a page that displays a blog post, the blog post itself is the epicenter. Not the categories in the sidebar, not the header at the top, not the comment form at the bottom, but the actual blog post unit. Without the blog post unit, the page isn't a blog post.

Only when that unit is complete would you begin to think about the second most critical element on the page. Then after the second most critical element, you'd move on to the third, and so on. That's epicenter design.

Epicenter design eschews the tradtional "let's build the frame then drop the content in" model. In that process, the page shape is built, then the nav is included, then the marketing "stuff" is inserted, and then, finally, the core functionality, the actual purpose of the page, is poured in to whatever space remains. It's a backwards process that takes what should be the top priority and saves it for the end.

Epicenter design flips that process and allows you to focus on what really matters on day one. Essentials first, extras second. The result is a more friendly, focused, usable screen for customers. Plus, it allows you to start the dialogue between designer and developer right away instead of waiting for all aspects of the page to fall in line first.

Three State Solution

Design for regular, blank, and error states

For each screen, you need to consider three possible states:

Regular
The screen people see when everything's
working fine and your app is flush with data.

Blank
The screen people see when using the app
for the first time, before data is entered.

Error
The screen people see when something goes wrong.

The regular state is a no-brainer. This is the screen where
you'll spend most of your time. But don't forget to invest
time on the other states too (see the following essays for
more on this).

The Blank Slate

Set expectations with a thoughtful first-run experience

Ignoring the blank slate stage is one of the biggest mistakes you can make. The blank slate is your app's first impression and you never get a second...well, you know.

The problem is that when designing a UI, it's usually flush with data. Designers always fill templates with data. Every list, every post, every field, every nook and cranny has stuff in it. And that means the screen looks and works great.

However, the natural state of the app is one that's devoid of data. When someone signs up, they start with a blank slate. Much like a weblog, it's up to them to populate it – the overall look and feel doesn't take shape until people enter their data: posts, links, comments, hours, sidebar info, or whatever.

Unfortunately, the customer decides if an application is worthy at this blank slate stage – the stage when there's the least amount of information, design, and content on which to judge the overall usefulness of the application. When you fail to design an adequate blank slate, people don't know what's missing because everything is missing.

Yet most designers and developers still take this stage for granted. They fail to spend a lot of time designing for the blank slate because when they develop/use the app, it's full of data that they've entered for testing purposes. They don't even encounter the blank slate. Sure, they may log-in as a new person a few times, but the majority of their time is spent swimming in an app that is full of data.
What should you include in a helpful blank slate?

Use it as an opportunity to insert quick tutorials and help blurbs.

Give a sample screenshot of the page populated with data so people know what to expect (and why they should stick around).

Explain how to get started, what the screen will eventually look like, etc.

Answer key questions that first-time viewers will ask: What is this page? What do I do now? How will this screen look once it's full?

Set expectations and help reduce frustration, intimidation, and overall confusion.

First impressions are crucial. If you fail to design a thoughtful blank slate, you'll create a negative (and false) impression of your application or service.

You Never Get A Second Chance...

Another aspect of the Mac OS X UI that I think has been tremendously influenced by [Steve] Jobs is the setup and first-run experience. I think Jobs is keenly aware of the importance of first impressions...I think Jobs looks at the first-run experience and thinks, it may only be one-thousandth of a user's overall experience with the machine, but it's the most important one-thousandth, because it's the first one-thousandth, and it sets their expectations and initial impression.

-John Gruber, author and web developer (from Interview with John Gruber)

Get Defensive

Design for when things go wrong

Let's admit it: Things will go wrong online. No matter how carefully you design your app, no matter how much testing you do, customers will still encounter problems. So how do you handle these inevitable breakdowns? With defensive design.

Defensive design is like defensive driving. The same way drivers must always be on the lookout for slick roads, reckless drivers, and other dangerous scenarios, site builders must constantly search for trouble spots that cause visitors confusion and frustration. Good site defense can make or break the customer experience.

We could fill a separate book with all the things we have to say about defensive design. In fact, we already have. "Defensive Design for the Web" is the title and it's a great resource for anyone who wants to learn how to improve error screens and other crisis points.

Remember: Your app may work great 90% of the time. But if you abandon customers in their time of need, they're unlikely to forget it.

Context Over Consistency

What makes sense here may not make sense there

Should actions be buttons or links? It depends on the action. Should a calendar view be in list-form or grid-form? It depends where it's being shown and how long the time period is. Does every global navigation link need to be on every page? Do you need a global search bar everywhere? Do you need the same exact footer on each page? The answer: "It depends."

That's why context is more important than consistency. It's OK to be inconsistent if your design makes more sense that way. Give people just what matters. Give them what they need when they need it and get rid of what they don't. It's better to be right than to be consistent.

Intelligent Inconsistency

Consistency is not necessary. For years, students of UI and UX have been taught that consistency in the interface is one of the cardinal rules of interface design. Perhaps that holds in software, but on the Web, it's just not true. What matters on the Web is whether, on each individual page, the user can quickly and easily advance the next step in the process.

At Creative Good, we call it "intelligent inconsistency": making sure that each page in the process gives users exactly what they need at that point in the process. Adding superfluous nav elements, just because they're consistent with the rest of the site, is just silly.

-Mark Hurst, founder of Creative Good and creator
of Goovite.com (from The Page Paradigm)

Copywriting is Interface Design

Every letter matters

Copywriting is interface design. Great interfaces are written. If you think every pixel, every icon, every typeface matters, then you also need to believe every letter matters. When you're writing your interface, always put yourself in the shoes of the person who's reading your interface. What do they need to know? How you can explain it succinctly and clearly?

Do you label a button Submit or Save or Update or New or Create? That's copywriting. Do you write three sentences or five? Do you explain with general examples or with details? Do you label content New or Updated or Recently Updated or Modified? Is it There are new messages: 5 or There are 5 new messages or is it 5 or five or messages or posts? All of this matters.

You need to speak the same language as your audience too. Just because you're writing a web app doesn't mean you can get away with technical jargon. Think about your customers and think about what those buttons and words mean to them. Don't use acronyms or words that most people don't understand. Don't use internal lingo. Don't sound like an engineer talking to another engineer. Keep it short and sweet. Say what you need to and no more.

Good writing is good design. It's a rare exception where words don't accompany design. Icons with names, form fields with examples, buttons with labels, step by step instructions in a process, a clear explanation of your refund policy. These are all interface design.

One Interface

Incorporate admin functions into the public interface

Admin screens – the screens used to manage preferences, people, etc. – have a tendency to look like crap. That's because the majority of development time is spent on the public-facing interface instead.

To avoid crappy-admin-screen syndrome, don't build separate screens to deal with admin functions. Instead, build these functions (i.e. edit, add, delete) into the regular application interface.

If you have to maintain two separate interfaces (i.e. one for regular folks and one for admins), both will suffer. In effect, you wind up paying the same tax twice. You're forced to repeat yourself and that means you increase the odds of getting sloppy. The fewer screens you have to worry about, the better they'll turn out.

No Separate Interface

The application is everything. Anything that can be changed, added, or adjusted can be done directly through the management area of the application. This allows us to see exactly what our customers see to help them through any problems or questions that they have. And our customers don't have to worry about logging into a separate interface to do different tasks. One minute they might be dealing with appointments for their clients and the next minute they might have to add a new employee. They can't be bothered with jumping between different applications and maintaining a consistent interface they're able to adapt to the application even quicker.

-Edward Knittel, Director of Sales and Marketing, KennelSource

Code

Less Software

Keep your code as simple as possible

You'd think that twice as much code would make your software only twice as complex. But actually, **each time you increase the amount of code, your software grows *exponentially* more complicated.** Each minor addition, each change, each interdependency, and each preference has a cascading effect. Keep adding code recklessly and, before you know it, you'll have created the dreaded Big Ball of Mud.

The way you fight this complexity is with less software. Less software means less features, less code, less waste.

The key is to restate any hard problem that requires a lot of software into a simple problem that requires much less. You may not be solving exactly the same problem but that's alright. Solving 80% of the original problem for 20% of the effort is a major win. The original problem is almost never so bad that it's worth five times the effort to solve it.

Less software means you put away the crystal ball. Instead of trying to predict future problems, you deal only with the problems of today. Why? Fears you have about tomorrow often never come to fruition. Don't bog yourself down trying to solve these phantom issues.

From the beginning, we've designed our products around the concept of less software. Whenever possible, we chop up hard problems into easy ones. We've found solutions to easy problems are not only easier to implement and support, they're easier to understand and easier to use. It's all part of how we differentiate ourselves from competitors; Instead of trying to build products that do more, we build products that do less.

Less software is easier to manage.

Less software reduces your codebase and that means less maintenance busywork (and a happier staff).

Less software lowers your cost of change so you can adapt quickly. You can change your mind without having to change boatloads of code.

Less software results in fewer bugs.

Less software means less support.

Which features you choose to include or omit have a lot to do with less software too. Don't be afraid to say no to feature requests that are hard to do. Unless they're absolutely essential, save time/effort/confusion by leaving them out.

Slow down too. Don't take action on an idea for a week and see if it still seems like a great idea after the initial buzz wears off. The extra marinading time will often help your brain come up with an easier solution.

Encourage programmers to make counteroffers. You want to hear: "The way you suggested will take 12 hours. But there's a way I can do it that will only take one hour. It won't do X but it will do Y." Let the software push back. Tell programmers to fight for what they think is the best way.

Also, search for detours around writing more software. Can you change the copy on the screen so that it suggests an alternate route to customers that doesn't require a change in the software model? For example, can you suggest that people upload images of a specific size instead of doing the image manipulation on the server side?

For every feature that makes it into your app, ask yourself: Is there a way this can be added that won't require as much software? Write just the code you need and no more. Your app will be leaner and healthier as a result.

There is No CODE That is More Flexible Than NO Code!

The "secret" to good software design wasn't in knowing what to put into the code; it was in knowing what to leave OUT! It was in recognizing where the hard-spots and soft-spots were, and knowing where to leave space/room rather than trying to cram in more design.

-Brad Appleton, software engineer (from There is No
CODE that is more flexible than NO Code!)

Complexity Does Not Scale Linearly With Size

The most important rule of software engineering is also the least known: Complexity does not scale linearly with size...A 2000 line program requires more than twice as much development time as one half the size.

-The Ganssle Group (from Keep It Small)

Optimize for Happiness

Choose tools that keep your team excited and motivated

A happy programmer is a productive programmer. That's why we optimize for happiness and you should too. Don't just pick tools and practices based on industry standards or performance metrics. Look at the intangibles: Is there passion, pride, and craftmanship here? Would you truly be happy working in this environment eight hours a day?

This is especially important for choosing a programming language. Despite public perception to the contrary, they are not created equal. While just about any language can create just about any application, the right one makes the effort not merely possible or bearable, but pleasant and invigorating. It's all about making the little details of daily work enjoyable.

Happiness has a cascading effect. Happy programmers do the right thing. They write simple, readable code. They take clean, expressive, readable, elegant approaches. They have fun.

We found programming bliss in the language Ruby and passed it on to other developers with our framework Rails. Both share a mission statement to optimize for humans and their happiness. We encourage you to give that combination a spin.

In summary, your team needs to work with tools they love. We've talked here in terms of programming languages, but the concept holds true for applications, platforms, and anything else. Choose the fuse that gets people excited. You'll generate excitement and motivation and a better product as a result.

The kinds of engineers you want

The number one reason I wanted to build our app using Ruby on Rails is that it is so elegant, productive, and beautifully designed. It tends to attract the kind of engineers who care about just those sort of things...those are exactly the kinds of engineers you want on your team because they create the kind of beautiful, elegant and productive software you need to win the market."

-Charles Jolley, Managing Director at Nisus Software (from Signal vs. Noise)

Code Speaks

Listen when your code pushes back

Listen to your code. It will offer suggestions. It will push back. It will tell you where the pitfalls reside. It will suggest new ways to do things. It will help you stick to a model of less software.

Is a new feature requiring weeks of time and thousands of lines of code? That's your code telling you there's probably a better way. Is there a simple way to code something in one hour instead of a complicated way that will take ten hours? Again, that's your code guiding you. Listen.

Your code can guide you to fixes that are cheap and light. Pay attention when an easy path emerges. Sure, the feature that's easy to make might not be exactly the same as the feature you originally had in mind but so what? If it works well enough and gives you more time to work on something else, it's a keeper.

....

Listen up

Don't worry about design, if you listen to your code a good design will appear...Listen to the technical people. If they are complaining about the difficulty of making changes, then take such complaints seriously and give them time to fix things.

-Martin Fowler, Chief Scientist, ThoughtWorks (from Is Design Dead?)

If Programmers Got Paid To Remove Code...

If programmers got paid to remove code from sofware instead
of writing new code, software would be a whole lot better.

*-Nicholas Negroponte, Wiesner Professor of Media Technology at the
Massachusetts Institute of Technology and founding chairman of MIT's
Media Laboratory (from And, the rest of the (AIGA Conference) story)*

Manage Debt

Pay off your code and design "bills"

We usually think of debt in terms of money but it comes in other forms too. You can easily build up code and design debt.

Hack together some bad code that's functional but still a bit hairy and you're building up debt. Throw together a design that's good enough but not really good and you've done it again.

It's OK to do this from time to time. In fact, it's often a needed technique that helps you do the whole Get-Real-ASAP-thing. But you still need to recognize it as debt and pay it off at some point by cleaning up the hairy code or redesigning that so-so page.

The same way you should regularly put aside some of your income for taxes, regularly put aside some time to pay off your code and design debt. If you don't, you'll just be paying interest (fixing hacks) instead of paying down the principal (and moving forward).

Open Doors

Get data out into the world via RSS, APIs, etc.

Don't try to lock-in your customers. Let them get their information when they want it and how they want it.

To do that, you've got to **give up the idea of sealing in data. Instead, let it run wild**. Give people access to their information via RSS feeds. Offer APIs that let third-party developers build on to your tool. When you do, you make life more convenient for customers and expand the possibilities of what your app can do.

People used to think of RSS feeds as merely a good way to keep track of blogs or news sites. Feeds have more power than that though. They also provide a great way for customers to stay up to date on the changing content of an app without having to log in repeatedly. With Basecamp feeds, customers can pop the URL into a newsreader and keep an eye on project messages, to-do lists, and milestones without having to constantly check in at the site.

APIs let developers build add-on products for your app that can turn out to be invaluable. For example, Backpack supplies an API which Chipt Productions used to build a Mac OS X Dashboard widget. The widget lets people add and edit reminders, list items, and more from the desktop. Customers have raved to us about this widget and some have even said it was the key factor in getting them to use Backpack.

Other good examples of companies letting data run free in order to get a boomerang effect:

The **Google Maps API** has spawned interesting mash-ups that let people cull information from another source (e.g. apartment listings) and plot that data on a map.

Linkrolls offer a way for people to get their latest del.icio.us bookmarks displayed on their own sites.

Flickr allows other businesses access to commercial APIs so customers can buy photo books, posters, DVD backups, and stamps. "The goal is to open it up completely and give you the biggest variety of choices when it comes to doing things with your photos," says Stewart Butterfield of Flickr.

A Widget Makes the Difference

When 37signals released Backpack a while back, my first impression was...eh.

So it was around the time that Chipt Productions released a Backpack widget for Tiger – which was too cool not to download and try – that I gave Backpack a second look. The result? Quite a difference.

Now whenever an idea hits, I pop up the widget, type, and submit – done. Email arrives with something I want to check out? Pop up the widget, type, and submit – done. The widget is an immediate brain dump readily available on each Mac I use. And because everything is web based, there isn't any version control or syncing – just the fluid input of content without having to be concerned about where it's going or how I'll access it later.

-Todd Dominey, founder, Dominey Design (from Trying on Backpack)

Words

There's Nothing Functional about a Functional Spec

Don't write a functional specifications document

These blueprint docs usually wind up having almost nothing to do with the finished product. Here's why:

Functional specs are fantasies

They don't reflect reality. An app is not real until builders are building it, designers are designing it, and people are using it. Functional specs are just words on paper.

Functional specs are about appeasement

They're about making everyone feel involved and happy which, while warm and fuzzy, isn't all that helpful. They're never about making tough choices and exposing costs, things that need to happen to build a great app.

Functional specs only lead to an illusion of agreement

A bunch of people agreeing on paragraphs of text isn't a true agreement. Everyone may be reading the same thing but they're thinking something different. This inevitably comes out later on: "Wait, that's not what I had in mind." "Huh? That's not how we described it." "Yes it was and we all agreed on it – you even signed off on it." You know the drill.

Functional specs force you to make the most important decisions when you have the least information

You know the least about something when you begin to build it. The more you build it, the more you use it, the more you know it. That's when you should be making decisions – when you have more information, not less.

Functional specs lead to feature overload

There's no pushback during spec phase. There's no cost to writing something down and adding another bullet point. You can please someone who's a pain by adding their pet feature. And then you wind up designing to those bullet points, not to humans. And that's how you wind up with an overloaded site that's got 30 tabs across the top of the screen.

Functional specs don't let you evolve, change,and reassess

A feature is signed off and agreed on. Even if you realize during development that it's a bad idea, you're stuck with it. Specs don't deal with the reality that once you start building something, everything changes.

So what should you do in place of a spec? Go with a briefer alternative that moves you toward something real.

Write a one page story about what the app needs to do. Use plain language and make it quick. If it takes more than a page to explain it, then it's too complex. This process shouldn't take more than one day.

Then begin building the interface – the interface will be the alternative to the functional spec. Draw some quick and simple paper sketches. Then start coding it into HTML. Unlike paragraphs of text that are open to alternate interpretations, interface designs are common ground that everyone can agree on.

Confusion disappears when everyone starts using the same screens. Build an interface everyone can start looking at, using, clicking through, and "feeling" before you start worrying about back-end code. Get yourself in front of the customer experience as much as possible.

Forget about locked-in specs. They force you to make big, key decisions too early in the process. Bypass the spec phase and you'll keep change cheap and stay flexible.

Useless Specs

A "spec" is close to useless. I have never seen a spec that was both big enough to be useful and accurate.

And I have seen lots of total crap work that was based on specs. It's the single worst way to write software, because it by definition means that the software was written to match theory, not reality.

-Linus Torvalds, creator of Linux (from: Linux: Linus On Specifications)

Fight the blockers

I found the people insisting on extensive requirements documents before starting any design were really 'blockers' just trying to slow the process down (and usually people with nothing to contribute on design or innovative thinking).

All our best work was done with a few concepts in our heads about improving a site, doing a quick prototype (static), changing the design a bit and then building a live prototype with real data. After kicking the tires on this prototype, we usually had a real project in motion and good result.

-Mark Gallagher, corporate intranet developer (from Signal vs. Noise)

Don't Do Dead Documents

Eliminate unnecessary paperwork

Avoiding functional specs is a good start but don't stop there; Prevent excess paperwork everywhere. Unless a document is actually going to morph into something real, don't produce it.

Build, don't write. If you need to explain something, try mocking it up and prototyping it rather than writing a long-winded document. An actual interface or prototype is on its way to becoming a real product. A piece of paper, on the other hand, is only on its way to the garbage can.

Here's an example: If a wireframe document is destined to stop and never directly become the actual design, don't bother doing it. If the wireframe starts as a wireframe and then morphs into the actual design, go for it.

Documents that live separately from your application are worthless. They don't get you anywhere. Everything you do should evolve into the real thing. If a document stops before it turns real, it's dead.

No One's Going to Read It

I can't even count how many multi-page product specifications or business requirement documents that have languished, unread, gathering dust nearby my dev team while we coded away, discussing problems, asking questions and user-testing as we went. I've even worked with developers who've spent hours writing long, descriptive emails or coding standards documents that also went unread.

Webapps don't move forward with copious documentation. Software development is a constantly shifting, iterative process that involves interaction, snap decisions, and impossible-to-predict issues that crop up along the way. None of this can or should be captured on paper.

Don't waste your time typing up that long visionary tome; no one's going to read it. Take consolation in the fact that if you give your product enough room to grow itself, in the end it won't resemble anything you wrote about anyway.

-Gina Trapani, web developer and editor of Lifehacker,
the productivity and software guide

Tell Me a Quick Story

Write stories, not details

If you do find yourself requiring words to explain a new feature or concept, write a brief story about it. Don't get into the technical or design details, just tell a quick story. Do it in a human way, like you would in normal conversation.

It doesn't need to be an essay. Just give the flow of what happens. And if you can include the brief story in context with screens you are developing, all the better.

Stick to the experience instead of getting hung up on the details. Think strategy, not tactics. The tactics will fall into place once you begin building that part of your app. Right now you just want to get a story going that will initiate conversation and get you on the right track.

Use Real Words

Insert actual text instead of lorem ipsum

Lorem ipsum dolor is a trusted friend of designers. Dummy text helps people get what the design will look like once it's fleshed out. But dummy text can be dangerous too.

Lorem ipsum changes the way copy is viewed. It reduces text-based content to a visual design element – a shape of text – instead of what it should be: valuable information someone is going to have to enter and/or read. Dummy text means you won't see the inevitable variations that show up once real information is entered. It means you won't know what it's like to fill out forms on your site. Dummy text is a veil between you and reality.

You need real copy to know how long certain fields should be. You need real copy to see how tables will expand or contract. You need real copy to know what your app truly looks like.

As soon as you can, use real and relevant words. If your site or application requires data input, enter the real deal. And actually type in the text – don't just paste it in from another source. If it's a name, type a real name. If it's a city, type a real city. If it's a password, and it's repeated twice, type it twice.

Sure, it's easier to just run down the forms and fill the fields with garbage ("asdsadklja" "123usadfjasld" "snaxn-2q9e7") in order to plow through them quickly. But that's not real. That's not what your customers are going to do. Is it really smart to take a shortcut when customers are forced to take the long road? When you just enter fake copy in rapid-fire fashion, you don't know what it really feels like to fill out that form.

Do as your customers do and you'll understand them better. When you understand them better, and feel what they feel, you'll build a better interface.

Lorem Ipsum Garbage

By not having the imagination to imagine what the content "might" be, a design consideration is lost. Meaning becomes obfuscated because "it's just text", understandability gets compromised because nobody realized that this text stuff was actually meant to be read. Opportunities get lost because the lorem ipsum garbage that you used instead of real content didn't suggest opportunities. The text then gets made really small, because, it's not meant to be used, we might as well create loads of that lovely white space.

-Tom Smith, designer and developer (from I hate Lorem Ipsum and Lorem Ipsum Users)

Personify Your Product

What is your product's personality type?

Think of your product as a person. What type of person do you want it to be? Polite? Stern? Forgiving? Strict? Funny? Deadpan? Serious? Loose? Do you want to come off as paranoid or trusting? As a know-it-all? Or modest and likable?

Once you decide, always keep those personality traits in mind as the product is built. Use them to guide the copywriting, the interface, and the feature set. Whenever you make a change, ask yourself if that change fits your app's personality.

Your product has a voice – and it's talking to your customers 24 hours a day.

Pricing and Signup

Free Samples

Easy On, Easy Off

Silly Rabbit, Tricks are for Kids

A Softer Bullet

Free Samples

Give something away for free

It's a noisy world out there. In order to get people to notice you amid the din, give something away for free.

Smart companies know giving away freebies is a great way to lure in customers. Look at Apple. They offer iTunes software for free in order to build demand for the iPod and the iTunes music store. In the offline world, retail outlets do the same. Starbucks says a new purchase is stimulated for every five beverage samples they give away to customers. Not too shabby.

For us, Writeboard and Ta-da list are completely free apps that we use to get people on the path to using our other products. Also, we always offer some sort of free version of all our apps.

We want people to experience the product, the interface, the usefulness of what we've built. Once they're hooked, they're much more likely to upgrade to one of the paying plans (which allow more projects or pages and gives people access to additional features like file uploading and SSL data encryption).

Bite-size chunks

Make bite-size chunks: Devise specialized, smaller offerings to get customers to bite. Resolve to sub-divide at least one product or service into bite-size chunks that are inexpensive, easy or fun.

-Ben McConnell and Jackie Huba, authors of Church of the Customer Blog
(from What is customer evangelism?)

Give Away Your Hit Single

Consider giving one of your songs (per-album) as a free promotional download to the world – to be like the movie trailer – like the hit single sent to radio – the song that makes people want to go buy your music.

Don't worry about piracy for this song. Let people play it, copy it, share it, give it away. Have the confidence that if the world heard it, they will pay for more.

-Derek Sivers, president and programmer, CD Baby
and HostBaby (from Free Promo Track)

Easy On, Easy Off

Make signup and cancellation a painless process

Make it as easy as possible to get in – and get out – of
your app.

If I'm a customer that wants to use your app, it should be
a painless, no-brainer process. Provide a big, clear, signup
button that pops and put it on each page of your marketing site. Tell folks how easy it is: "From sign-up to login in
just 1 minute!"

There should always be a free option so customers can
demo the app without entering credit card information.
Some of our competitors require a call back, an appoint-
ment, or a special password in order to try their product.
What's the deal with that? We let anyone try our apps for
free at any time.

Keep the signup form as short as possible. Don't ask for
stuff you don't need and don't throw a long daunting form
at people.

The same principles hold true for the cancellation process.
You never want to "trap" people inside your product.
While we're sorry when people decide to cancel their Basecamp account, we never make that process intimidating or
confusing. "Cancel my account" is a link that's clear as day
on a person's account page. There shouldn't be any email
to send, special form to fill out, or questions to answer.

Also, make sure people can get their data out if they decide to leave. We make sure customers can easily export all messages and comments in XML format at any time. It's their data and they should be able to do with it what they want.

This is crucial because giving people control over their information builds trust. You're giving them a bridge to their data island. You're allowing them to leave without penalty if they find a better offer. It's the right thing to do and it builds goodwill.

....

Exit with Ease

Don't hold users against their will. If they want to leave, let them pick up with all of the content they created while they were on your site and leave...for free...You have to let the barn door open and focus on keeping your customers fed, so they want to come back, instead of coming back because they're stuck.

-Charlie O'Donnell, analyst, Union Square Ventures
(from 10 Steps to a Hugely Successful Web 2.0 Company)

Silly Rabbit, Tricks are for Kids

Avoid long-term contracts, sign-up fees, etc.

No one likes long term contracts, early termination fees, or one-time set-up fees. So avoid them. Our products bill on a month-to-month basis. There's no contract to sign and you can cancel at any time without penalty. And there are never any set-up fees.

Don't try to find "tricky" ways to get more cash. Earn it.

A Softer Bullet

Soften the blow of bad news with advance notice and grandfather clauses

Need to deliver bad news like a price increase? Make it as painless as possible by giving folks plenty of advance notice. Also, consider a grandfather period that exempts existing customers for a certain period of time. These folks are your bread and butter and you want to make them feel valued, not gouged.

Promotion

Hollywood Launch

Go from teaser to preview to launch

If an app launches in a forest and there's no one there to use it, does it make a noise? The point here is that if you launch your app without any pre-hype, people aren't going to know about it.

To build up buzz and anticipation, go with a Hollywood-style launch: 1) Teaser, 2) Preview, and 3) Launch.

Teaser

A few months ahead of time, start dropping hints. Let people know what you're working on. Post a logo. Post to your blog about the development. Stay vague but plant the seed. Also, get a site up where you can collect emails from folks who are interested.

At this stage, you should also start seducing mavens and insiders. These are the folks on the cutting edge. They're the tastemakers. Appeal to their vanity and status as ahead-of-the-curvers. Tell them they're getting an exclusive sneak preview. If a site like Boing Boing, Slashdot, or Digg links up your app, you'll get loads of traffic and followers. Plus, your page rank at Google will go up too.

Preview

A few weeks ahead of launch, start previewing features. Give people behind-the-scenes access. Describe the theme of the product. For Basecamp, we posted screenshots and highlighted reminders, milestones, and other features.

Also, tell people about the ideas and principles behind the app. For Backpack, we posted our manifesto before launch. This got people thinking and talking about the app.

You can also offer some special "golden tickets" to a few people so they can start using the app early. You'll get the benefit of having some beta testers while they'll feel that special glow that people get from being early adopters.

And again, encourage people to sign up so you've got a foundation of emails to blitz once you launch. By the time we launch our apps, we have thousands of emails to ping which is a big help in gaining traction.

Launch

It's release time. Now people can actually go to the "theater" and see your app. Get emails out to those who signed up. Launch your full marketing site. Spread the gospel as much as possible. Get blogs to link to you. Post about your progress: How many people have signed up? What updates/tweaks have you made? Show momentum and keep at it.

The Road to Launch Day

As soon as we knew Blinksale was really going to happen, we began floating some teasers to our mailing list. These are people who have asked to receive information from us about our projects. These are our fans, if you will. If you already have permission to talk to a group of people, they are the best place to start.

The second thing we did is get permission to talk to more people about our product. About six weeks before the Blinksale launch we put up a teaser page at our website that proclaimed the coming of an easier way to send invoices online. The page gave just enough information to build excitement and suspense, without giving away sensitive details that needed to remain confidential. Prominently displayed on the page was a newsletter subscription form, requiring nothing but an email (keep it simple) so that those interested could be notified when the product launched.

We spread the word to a dozen or so friends and colleagues that we felt would be interested in the product as well, and they began to spread the word about the teaser page through their blogs and websites. Within a few days, we had thousands on our mailing list. These were extremely important people – people who are asking to learn more about our product and who wanted to know when we launched.

Finally, about two weeks before we launched, we invited a handful of friends, colleagues, and industry mavens to help us beta test Blinksale. This allowed us to get the product in front of people we felt could benefit from its use and who could help us spread the word about the product when we launched. It's important to note that we didn't force anyone to use or write about the product. We simply wanted it to be seen and wanted people to talk about it when it launched. In the end, if you're going to build buzz this way, you better be sure your product can deliver. Otherwise, it's like clouds without rain.

When launch day arrived, we sent an email to our mailing list, notified our blogging friends, and encouraged our beta testers to speak their minds. And to our great delight, the effort paid big dividends. Shortly after launch tens of thousands had visited our site and thousands of those had signed up to use the product.

-Josh Williams, founder, Blinksale

A Powerful Promo Site

Build an ace promotional site that introduces people to your product

The best promotional tool is a great product. Word will get out if you've got an app that people find really useful.

Still, you need an ace promotional site too. What should you include on this site? Some ideas:

Overview: Explain your app and its benefits.

Tour: Guide people through various features.

Screen captures and videos: Show people what the app actually looks like and how to use it.

Manifesto: Explain the philosophy and ideas behind it.

Case Studies: Provide real life examples that show what's possible.

Buzz: Testimonial quotes from customers, reviews, press.

Forum: Offer a place for members of the community to help one another.

Pricing & Sign-up: Get people into your app as quickly as possible.

Weblog: Blogs keep your site fresh with news, tips, etc.

Ride the Blog Wave

Blogging can be more effective than advertising (and it's a hell of a lot cheaper)

Advertising is expensive. And evaluating the effectiveness of various types of advertising can wind up being even more expensive than the advertising itself. When you don't have the time or money to go the traditional advertising route, consider the promote-via-blog route instead.

Start off by creating a blog that not only touts your product but offers helpful advice, tips, tricks, links, etc. Our Signal vs. Noise blog gets thousands of unique readers a week thanks to the helpful, informative, and interesting bits and anecdotes we post on a daily basis.

So when it came time to promote our first product, Basecamp, we started there. We got the word out on SvN and it started to spread. Folks like Jason Kottke, the BoingBoingers, Jim Coudal, and a variety of other people with popular blogs helped raise the visibility and things took off.

Ta-da Lists is another great example of the power of blog-based marketing. We launched Ta-da with a single post on Signal vs. Noise, and a few weeks later it had been mentioned on over 200 blogs and over 12,000 people had signed up for their own Ta-da account. Word about Backpack spread even faster. Within 24 hours of launch, more than than 10,000 signed up.

Solicit Early

Get advance buzz and signups going ASAP

We've already touched on it but it bears repeating: Get some sort of site up and start collecting emails as soon as possible. Pick your domain name and put up a logo and maybe a sentence or two that describes, or at least hints at, what your app will do. Then let people give you their email address. Now you're on your way to having a foundation of folks ready and waiting to be notified of your launch.

Promote Through Education

Share your knowledge with the world

When a teacher appears as a contestant on Jeopardy, Alex Trebek often comments that it's a "noble profession." He's right. There's definitely something wonderful and rewarding about sharing your knowledge with others. And when the subject you're teaching is your app, it serves a dual purpose: **You can give something back to the community that supports you and score some nice promotional exposure at the same time.**

As a promotional technique, education is a soft way to get your name – and your product's name – in front of more people. And instead of a hard sell "buy this product" approach, you're getting attention by providing a valuable service. That creates positive buzz that traditional marketing tactics can't match. People who you educate will become your evangelists.

Education can come in many forms. Post tips and tricks at your site that people will want to share with others. Speak at conferences and stay afterwards to meet and greet with attendees. Conduct workshops so curious fans can learn more and talk to you in the flesh. Give interviews to publications. Write articles that share helpful information. And write books. ;)

An example from our own history is the Yellow Fade Technique, a method we invented to subtly spotlight a recently changed area on a page. We wrote a post about it on Signal vs. Noise. That post made the rounds and got thousands and thousands of page views (to this day it's doing huge traffic).

The post worked on both an educational and a promotional level. A lesson was learned and a lot of people who never would have known about our products were exposed to them.

Another example: During our development of Ruby on Rails, we decided to make the infrastructure open source. It turned out to be a wise move. We gave something back to the community, built up goodwill, garnered recognition for our team, received useful feedback, and began receiving patches and contributions from programmers all over the world.

Teaching is all about good karma. You're paying it forward. You're helping others. You get some healthy promotion. And you can even bask in a bit of nobility. So what do you know that the world wants to hear about?

Pay It Forward

The articles and tips section of our blog is one of the most popular sections of our site. Passing on our knowledge about email marketing ensures our customers get the most out of our software. If they can provide a better service to their customers, then they're likely to get more business, which in turn creates more business for us – everyone wins.

Freely sharing our knowledge has also helped position us as experts in the industry and strengthened our relationship with existing customers. They know we care about the quality of their work. Finally, we get loads of targeted inbound traffic from search engines and bloggers who share our articles with their readers. These are people that would never have heard of our software had we not written that article.

-David Greiner, founder, Campaign Monitor

Creating Evangelists

The more that a company shares its knowledge, the more valuable it becomes. Companies that share their intellectual property and business processes with customers and partners are more likely to have their knowledge (or products) passed along to prospective customers. People tend to evangelize products and services they love, admire or find valuable.

-Ben McConnell and Jackie Huba, authors of Church of the Customer Blog (from Napsterize Your Knowledge: Give To Receive)

Teaching Leads to Passion

Those who teach stand the best chance of getting people to become passionate. And those with the most passionate users don't need an ad campaign when they've got user evangelists doing what evangelists do... talking about their passion.

-Kathy Sierra, author, Creating Passionate Users (from You can out-spend or out-teach)

Feature Food

They're hungry for it so serve it up

New or interesting features are a great way to generate buzz for your application. Special interest groups love to chew up "feature food" and spit it back out to the community. Alright, that's kind of an unpleasant analogy but you get the point.

For example, by using Ruby on Rails, a new development platform, we generated a ton of attention for Basecamp within the developer community.

The Ajax elements we used in our applications got lots of buzz and even led to Business 2.0 magazine naming 37signals a "key player in Ajax" alongside big names like Google, Yahoo, Microsoft, and Amazon.

Another example: Bloggers took notice of Basecamp's RSS support since it was one of the first business examples of RSS.

iCal integration, a seemingly minor feature, got us press on a ton of Mac-related sites which probably never would have mentioned the app otherwise.

Small teams have a leg up on integrating new ideas into software. While bigger companies have to deal with bureaucratic bottlenecks, you can rapidly implement new ideas and get attention for using them.

Riding the hype coattails of the technology du jour is an effective and cheap way to build your buzz. That said, don't go adding the latest obscure technology just to gain some notice. But if you are using something new or noteworthy, go ahead and spotlight it for special interest groups.

Track Your Logs

Study your logs to track buzz

You need to know who's talking about you. Check your logs and find out where the buzz is coming from. Who's linking to you? Who's bitching about you? Which blogs listed at Technorati, Blogdex, Feedster, Del.icio.us, and Daypop are hot on your trail?

Find out and then make your presence felt. Leave comments at those blogs. Thank people for posting links. Ask them if they want to be included on your special advance list so they'll be among the first to know about future releases, updates, etc. Collect positive praise and create a "buzz" page at your site. Testimonials are a great way to promote your app since third-party praise is more trustworthy to most people.

If the comments are negative, still pay attention. Show you're listening. Respond to critiques thoughtfully. Something like: "We appreciate the feedback but we did it this way because..." Or "You raise a good point and we're working on it." You'll soften up your critics and put a human face on your product. It's amazing how much a thoughtful comment on a blog can diffuse naysayers and even turn complainers into evangelists.

Inline Upsell

Promote upgrade opportunities inside the app

Everyone knows to pitch at the marketing site. But the sell shouldn't stop there. If you have a tiered pricing plan (or a free version of your app), don't forget to call out upgrade opportunities from within the product.

Tell folks that you'll remove barriers if they upgrade. For example, in Basecamp you can't upload files if you have a free account. When someone tries to upload a file, we don't just turn them away. We explain why file uploading isn't available and encourage them to upgrade to the paid version and explain why that's a good idea. The same approach is used to encourage existing customers to upgrade to a higher level account when they max out their current plan.

Existing customers are your best bet for sales. Don't be shy about trying to get repeat business from people who already know and use your product.

Name Hook

Give your app a name that's easy to remember

A big mistake a lot of people make is thinking their app's name needs to be ultradescriptive. Don't worry about picking a name that vividly describes your tool's purpose; That usually just leads to a generic, forgettable name. Basecamp is a better name than something like Project Management Center or ProjectExpress. Writeboard is better than CollaborEdit.

Also, don't focus group or committee-ize the naming process too much. Pick a name that's short, catchy, and memorable and then run with it.

And don't sweat it if you can't get the exact domain name you want. You can always be creative and get close with a couple of extra letters (e.g. backpackit.com or campfirenow.com).

Easy Does It

Doesn't the tech industry realize that thinking up catchy, self-explanatory names would ultimately benefit it in the same way? They'd sell more of whatever it was, because they wouldn't scare off consumers who think they're being kept out of the high-tech club by a bunch of arrogant engineers. The technology would catch on quicker, too. The new product would be easier to describe, easier to use and easier to buy – which, for the companies, means easier to sell.

-David Pogue, columnist, New York Times (from What's in a Product Name?)

Support

Feel The Pain

Tear down the walls between support and development

In the restaurant business, there's a world of difference between those working in the kitchen and those out front who deal with customers. It's important for both sides to understand and empathize with the other. That's why cooking schools and restaurants will often have chefs work out front as waiters so the kitchen staff can interact with customers and see what it's actually like on the front lines.

A lot of software developers have a similar split. Designers and programmers work in the "kitchen" while support handles the customers. Unfortunately, that means the software chefs never get to hear what customers are actually saying. That's problematic because listening to customers is the best way to get in tune with your product's strengths and weaknesses.

The solution? Avoid building walls between your customers and the development/design team. **Don't outsource customer support to a call center or third party.** Do it yourself. You, and your whole team, should know what your customers are saying. When your customers are annoyed, you need to know about it. You need to hear their complaints. You need to get annoyed too.

At 37signals, all of our support emails are answered personally by the people who actually build the product. Why? First off, it provides better support for customers. They're getting a response straight from the brain of someone who built the app. Also, it keeps us in touch with the people who use our products and the problems they're encountering. When they're frustrated, we're frustrated. We can say, "I feel your pain" and actually mean it.

It can be tempting to rely on statistical analysis to reveal your trouble spots. But stats aren't the same as voices. You need to eliminate as many buffers as possible between you and the real voices of your customers.

The front lines are where the action is. Get up there. Have your chefs work as waiters. Read customer emails, hear their frustrations, listen to their suggestions and learn from them.

Cut Out the Middle Man

Almost all Campaign Monitor development, support and marketing are performed by two people. Even if we're forced to expand the team, we'll never separate support from development. By personally responding to every request, we force ourselves to sit in our customers shoes and see things from their perspective.

It's important to understand why your customer needs something, not just what it is they need. That context often has a direct impact on how we design something. Cut out the middle man. It's much easier to give your customers what they want when your ears are that close to the ground.

I've discussed this setup with loads of people and the first response is often "shouldn't you just hire a junior to handle your support?" Put yourself in your customer's shoes. If you want your steak cooked just how you like it, would you rather talk to the bus boy or the chef that's actually cooking it?

-David Greiner, founder, Campaign Monitor

Zero Training

**Use inline help and FAQs so your product doesn't
require a manual or training**

You don't need a manual to use Yahoo or Google or
Amazon. So why can't you build a product that doesn't
require a manual? Strive to build a tool that requires zero
training.

How do you do this? Well, as we've mentioned before, you
start by keeping everything simple. The less complex your
app is, the less you'll need to help people out of the weeds.
After that, a great way to preempt support is by using
inline help and FAQs at potential points of confusion.

For example, we offer preemptive support on the screen
that allows people to upload their logo to Basecamp. Some
people experienced a problem where they would keep
seeing an old logo due to a browser-caching issue. So next
to the "submit your logo" area, we added a link to an FAQ
that instructed customers to force-reload their browsers in
order to see the new logo. Before we did this, we would
get 5 emails a day about this problem. Now we get none.

Answer Quick

Quick turnaround time on support queries should be a top priority

Customers light up when you answer their questions quickly. They're so used to canned responses that show up days later (if at all) that you can really differentiate yourself from competitors by offering a thoughtful response right away. During business hours, we answer 90% of all email support requests within 90 minutes – and often within a half-hour. And people love it.

Even if you don't have a perfect answer, say something. You can buy goodwill with a response that is delivered quickly in an open, honest way. If someone is complaining about an issue that can't be fixed immediately, tell them something like, "We hear what you're saying and we'll be working on it in the future." It's a great way to diffuse a potentially negative situation.

Customers appreciate directness and will often shift from angry to polite if you respond quickly and in a straight-shooting manner.

An Army of Many

How can a small team of just three developers create an innovative product and successfully compete with the big guys? The answer is to enlist an army of many.

Remember from your first day that your customers are your most important asset and that they are absolutely vital to your long-term success so treat your community of users like royalty. The way to compete with the big guys is by starting small and paying attention to every one of your customers.

It is your customers that will be the first to alert you of bugs, that will be the first to alert you of needs that have not been met and it is your first customers that will carry the flag and spread your message.

This does not mean that your product has to be perfect when you launch. Quite to the contrary, release early and often. However, when your customers encounter bugs, make sure to send a reply to them quickly thanking them for their input.

Customers don't expect your product to be perfect and they don't expect that all of their features will be implemented. However, customers do expect that you are listening and acknowledging that you care, so show that you care. This is one area where most large companies show a huge deficit so develop a sense of community early.

At Blinklist, every single customer email is answered, usually within the first hour (unless we happen to be asleep). We also have an online forum and we make sure that every single post and comment gets acknowledged.

Equally important, all of our developers receive our customer feedback and they are active participants in the online discussion forums. This way, we are slowly but surely building an active and loyal BlinkList community.

-Michael Reining, co-founder, MindValley & Blinklist

Tough Love

Be willing to say no to your customers

When it comes to feature requests, the customer is not always right. If we added every single thing our customers requested, no one would want our products.

If we obeyed every whim of our customers, Basecamp would have: comprehensive time tracking, comprehensive billing, comprehensive meeting scheduling, comprehensive calendaring, comprehensive dependency task systems, comprehensive instant message chatting, comprehensive wiki functionality, and comprehensive whatever-else-you-can-imagine.

Yet, the #1 request we get on customer surveys is to keep Basecamp simple.

Here's another example: Despite some complaints, we decided not to support IE 5 with our products. That was 7% of the market we were writing off. But we decided it was more important to worry about the other 93%. Fixing bugs and testing for IE 5 just isn't worth the time. We'd rather make a better product for everyone else.

As a software development company, you have to act as a filter. Not everything everyone suggests is the right answer. We consider all requests but the customer is not always right. There will be times when you just have to piss some people off. C'est la vie.

Related to this, it's critical that you as a development company love your product. And you won't love your product if it's filled with a bunch of stuff you don't agree with. That's yet another justification for vetoing customer requests that you don't believe are necessary.

In Fine Forum

Use forums or chat to let customers help each other

Forums and web-based group chat are a great way to let customers ask questions and help one another out. By eliminating the middleman – that's you – you provide an open stream of communication and save yourself time in the process.

At our product forums, customers post tips and tricks, feature requests, stories, and more. We pop in from time to time to offer some assistance but the forums are mainly a place for the community to help each other and share their experiences with the product.

You'll be surprised how much people want to help one another.

Publicize Your Screwups

Get bad news out there and out of the way

If something goes wrong, tell people. Even if they never saw it in the first place.

For example, Basecamp was down once for a few hours in the middle of the night. 99% of our customers never knew, but we still posted an "unexpected downtime" notice to our Everything Basecamp blog. We thought our customers deserved to know.

Here's a sample of what we post when something goes wrong: "We apologize for the downtime this morning – we had some database issues which caused major slowdowns and downtimes for some people. We've fixed the problem and are taking steps to make sure this doesn't happen again...Thanks for your patience and, once again, we're sorry for the downtime."

Be as open, honest, and transparent as possible. Don't keep secrets or hide behind spin. An informed customer is your best customer. Plus, you'll realize that most of your screwups aren't even that bad in the minds of your customers. Customers are usually happy to give you a little bit of breathing room as long as they know you're being honest with them.

A side note about delivering news, bad and good: When bad news comes, get it all out in the open at once. Good news, on the other hand, should be trickled out slowly. If you can prolong the good vibes, do it.

Be Swift, Direct, and Honest

It may sound strange, but the best-case scenario is when the company itself reports the bad news. This is proactive and prevents your company from being put in a weakened, defensive position.

-Greg Sherwin, Vice President of Application Technology, CNET, and Emily Avila, Principal, Calypso Communications (from A Primer for Crisis PR)

Post-Launch

One Month Tuneup

Keep the Posts Coming

Better, Not Beta

All Bugs Are Not Created Equal

Ride Out the Storm

Keep Up With the Joneses

Beware the Bloat Monster

Go With The Flow

One Month Tuneup

Issue a major update 30 days after launch

A quick update shows momentum. It shows you're listening. It shows you've got more tricks up your sleeve. It gives you a second wave of buzz. It reaffirms initial good feelings. It gives you something to talk about and others to blog about.

Knowing a quick upgrade is coming also lets you put the focus on the most crucial components before launch. Instead of trying to squeeze in a few more things, you can start by perfecting just the core feature set. Then you can "air out" the product in the real world. Once it's out there you can start getting customer feedback and you'll know which areas require attention next.

This baby-step approach worked well for Backpack. We launched the base product first and then, a few weeks later, added features like Backpack Mobile for handhelds and tagging since those things are what our customers told us they wanted most.

Keep the Posts Coming

Show your product is alive by keeping an ongoing product development blog post-launch

Don't stop blogging once you launch. Show your product is a living creature by keeping a dedicated blog that you update frequently (at least once a week, more often if you can).

Things to include:

FAQs

How-tos

Tips & tricks

New features, updates, & fixes

Buzz/press

A blog not only shows your app is alive, it makes your company seem more human. Again, don't be afraid to keep the tone friendly and personal. Small teams sometimes feel like they need to sound big and ultra-professional all the time. It's almost like a business version of the Napoleon Complex. Don't sweat sounding small. Revel in the fact that you can talk to customers like a friend.

It's Alive

A frequently-updated product blog is the best indicator that a webapp is in active development, that it's loved and that there's a light on at home. An abandoned product blog is a sign of an abandoned product, and says the people in charge are asleep at the wheel.

Keep the conversation going with your users on your product blog, and be transparent and generous with the information you share. Let your company's philosophies shine through. Openly link and discuss competitors. Hint at upcoming features and keep comments open for feedback.

A living product is one that's talking and listening to its users. A frequently-updated product blog promotes transparency, a sense of community and loyalty to your brand. Extra, free publicity is a bonus.

As editor at Lifehacker, I scan the product blogs of webapps I love continuously – like Google, Flickr, Yahoo, del.icio.us, and 37signals product blogs. I'm much more likely to mention them than webapps that send out one-sided press releases out of the blue and don't maintain an open conversation with their users and fans.

-Gina Trapani, web developer and editor of Lifehacker,
the productivity and software guide

Better, Not Beta

Don't use "beta" as a scapegoat

These days it feels like everything is in beta stage forever. That's a cop out. An interminable beta stage tells customers you're not really committed to rolling out a finished product. It says, "Use this, but if it's not perfect, it's not our fault."

Beta passes the buck to your customers. If you're not confident enough about your release then how can you expect the public to be? Private betas are fine, public betas are bullshit. If it's not good enough for public consumption don't give it to the public to consume.

Don't wait for your product to reach perfection. It's not gonna happen. Take responsibility for what you're releasing. Put it out and call it a release. Otherwise, you're just making excuses.

Beta is Meaningless

Blame Google, et al, for causing problems like this. For now, users have been trained by the aggregate of developers to think "beta" doesn't really mean anything.

> *-Mary Hodder, information architect and interaction designer (from The Definition of Beta)*

All the Time

Is it just me, or are we all in beta, all the time?

> *-Jim Coudal, founder, Coudal Partners*

All Bugs Are Not Created Equal

Prioritize your bugs (and even ignore some of them)

Just because you discover a bug in your product, doesn't mean it's time to panic. All software has bugs – it's just a fact of life.

You don't have to fix each bug instantly. Most bugs are annoying, not destroying. Annoyances can be tabled for a bit. Bugs that result in "it doesn't look right" errors or other misdemeanor miscues can safely be set aside for a while. If a bug destroys your database, though, you obviously need to fix it immediately.

Prioritize your bugs. How many people are affected? How bad is the problem? Does this bug deserve immediate attention or can it wait? What can you do right now that will have the greatest impact for the greatest number of people? Often times adding a new feature may even be more important to your app than fixing an existing bug.

Also, don't create a culture of fear surrounding bugs. Bugs happen. Don't constantly seek someone to blame. The last thing you want is an environment where bugs are shoved under the rug instead of openly discussed.

And remember what we said earlier about the importance of honesty. If customers complain about a bug, be straight up with them. Tell them you've noted the issue and are dealing with it. If it won't be addressed right away, tell why and explain that you're focusing on areas of the product that affect a greater number of people. Honesty is the best policy.

Ride Out the Storm

Wait until knee-jerk reactions to changes die down before taking action

When you rock the boat, there will be waves. After you introduce a new feature, change a policy, or remove something, knee-jerk reactions, often negative, will pour in.

Resist the urge to panic or rapidly change things in response. Passions flare in the beginning. But if you ride out this initial 24-48 hour period, things will usually settle down. Most people respond before they've really dug in and used whatever you've added (or gotten along with what you've removed). So sit back, take it all in, and don't make a move until some time has passed. Then you'll be able to offer a more reasoned response.

Also, remember that negative reactions are almost always louder and more passionate than positive ones. In fact, you may only hear negative voices even when the majority of your base is happy about a change. Make sure you don't foolishly backpedal on a necessary, but controversial, decision.

Keep Up With the Joneses

Subscribe to news feeds about your competitors

Subscribe to news feeds about both your product and your competitors (it's always wise to know the ways of one's enemy). Use services like PubSub, Technorati, Feedster, and others to stay up to date (for keywords, use company names and product names). With RSS, this constantly changing info will be delivered right to you so you're always up to speed.

Beware the Bloat Monster

More mature doesn't have to mean more complicated

As things progress, don't be afraid to resist bloat. The temptation will be to scale up. But it doesn't have to be that way. Just because something gets older and more mature, doesn't mean it needs to get more complicated.

You don't have to become an outer space pen that writes upside down. Sometimes it's OK to just be a pencil. You don't need to be a swiss-army knife. You can just be a screwdriver. You don't need to build a diving watch that's safe at 5,000 meters if your customers are land-lovers who just want to know what the time is.

Don't inflate just for the sake of inflating. That's how apps get bloated.

New doesn't always mean improved. Sometimes there's a point where you should just let a product be.

This is one of the key benefits to building web-based software instead of traditional desktop based software. Desktop software makers such as Adobe, Intuit, and Microsoft need to sell you new versions every year. And since they can't just sell you the same version, they have to justify the expense by adding new features. That's where the bloat begins.

With web-based software based on the subscription model, people pay a monthly fee to use the service. You don't need to keep upselling them by adding more and more and more, you just need to provide an ongoing valuable service.

Go With the Flow

Be open to new paths and changes in direction

Part of the beauty of a web app is its fluidity. You don't wrap it up in a box, ship it, and then wait years for the next release. You can tweak and change as you go along. Be open to the fact that your original idea may not be your best one.

Look at Flickr. It began as a multiplayer online game called The Game Neverending. Its creators soon realized the photo-sharing aspect of the game was a more plausible product than the game itself (which was eventually shelved). Be willing to admit mistakes and change course.

Be a surfer. Watch the ocean. Figure out where the big waves are breaking and adjust accordingly.

Conclusion

Start Your Engines
37signals Resources

Start Your Engines

Done!

Alright, you made it! Hopefully you're psyched to start Getting Real with your app. There really has never been a better time to make great software with minimal resources. With the right idea, passion, time, and skill, the sky's the limit.

A few closing thoughts:

Execution

Everyone can read a book. Everyone can come up with an idea. Everyone has a cousin that's a web designer. Everyone can write a blog. Everyone can hire someone to hack together some code.

The difference between you and everyone else will be how well you execute. Success is all about great execution.

For software, that means doing a lot of things right. You can't just have good writing but then fail to deliver on the promises in your prose. Clean interface design won't cut it if your code is full of hacks. A great app is worthless if poor promotion means no one ever knows about it. To score big, you have to combine all these elements.

The key is balance. If you tilt too far in one direction, you're headed for failure. Constantly seek out your weak links and focus on them until they're up to par.

People

It's worth reemphasizing the one thing that we think is the most important ingredient when it comes to building a successful web app: the people involved. Mantras, epicenter design, less software, and all these other wonderful ideas won't really matter if you don't have the right people on board to implement them.

You need people who are passionate about what they do. People who care about their craft – and actually think of it as a craft. People who take pride in their work, regardless of the monetary reward involved. People who sweat the details even if 95% of folks don't know the difference. People who want to build something great and won't settle for less. People who need people. OK, not really that last one but we couldn't resist throwing a little Streisand into the mix. Anyhow, when you find those people, hold onto them. In the end, the folks on your team will make or break your project – and your company.

More Than Just Software

It's also worth noting that the concept of Getting Real doesn't apply just to building a web app. Once you start grasping the ideas involved, you'll see them all over the place. Some examples:

Special ops forces, like the Green Berets or Navy Seals, use small teams and rapid deployment to accomplish tasks that other units are too big or too slow to get done.

The White Stripes embrace restraints by sticking to a simple formula: two people, streamlined songs, childlike drumming, keeping studio time to a minimum, etc.

Apple's iPod differentiates itself from competitors by not offering features like a built-in FM radio or a voice recorder.

Hurry up offenses in football pick up
big chunks of yards by eliminating the
"bureaucracy" of huddles and play-calling.

Rachael Ray bases her successful cookbooks and TV
show on the concept of 30-minute "Get Real Meals."

Ernest Hemingway and Raymond Carver used simple,
clear language yet still delivered maximum impact.

Shakespeare reveled in the limitations of sonnets,
fourteen-line lyric poems in iambic pentameter.

And on and on...

Sure, Getting Real is about building great software. But
there's no reason why it needs to stop there. Take these
ideas and try applying them to different aspects of your
life. You might just stumble upon some neat results.

Keep In Touch

Let us know how Getting Real works out for you. Send an
email to gettingreal@37signals.com.

Also, stay up to date with the latest offerings from
37signals by visiting Signal vs. Noise (www.37signals.
com/svn), our blog about Getting Real, usability, design,
and a bunch of other stuff.

And finally, there's more info at our main site
(www.37signals.com) and a special area we've dedicated
to Getting Real (getreal.37signals.com).

Thanks for reading and good luck!

37signals Resources

37signals site

http://www.37signals.com

Signal vs. Noise weblog

http://www.37signals.com/svn

Basecamp – Web-based project collaboration

http://www.basecamphq.com
Enter 5E8CPH3SMJ when you upgrade from a free to a
paying plan and save $10 on your first month.

Campfire – Web-based group chat for business

http://www.campfirenow.com

Backpack – Web-based information organizer

http://www.backpackit.com
SPECIAL OFFER: Enter JMPEZ7XDKT when you upgrade from
a free to a paying plan and save $10 on your first month.

Writeboard – Web-based collaborative writing

http://www.writeboard.com

Ta-da List – Web-based dead-simple to-do lists

http://www.tadalist.com

Ruby on Rails – Open-source web application framework

http://www.rubyonrails.org

Breinigsville, PA USA
21 February 2010
232886BV00001B/211/P